Dream Big. Live Bigger.

THE ACTOR'S
AUDITION GUIDE

to booking roles in film & television

ISBN: 9781676140108
Imprint: Independently published

PREFACE

Throughout my career, and my life I have been extremely fortunate to meet childhood idols and other mentors. They have given me their time, shared their knowledge, and offered me skills and information, creating opportunities like I never knew possible.

In each case, the resounding message has always been to make sure you share this information with the next generation. The pay it forward mindset of so many of my heroes and mentors has made a lasting impression on me and it has motivated me to not only pay it forward but to inspire others to do the same.

The other reason I felt compelled to write this book, was in response to meeting so many people who have been told not to chase their dreams because it is too hard, or not smart, or not safe, or not realistic.

I still remember, age 17, telling my mother I was going to be a professional actor and maybe a writer when I grew up. Her response? "Excellent. You should do what makes you happy. Just be good enough that someone will pay you because you can't live here forever." When I booked the role of Happy on ABC's Once Upon a Time, I probably took this advice too literally, but it also validated my Mom's initial advice. I am also pretty sure my Mom will always let me move home if I ever need it but this overwhelming vote of confidence set me on a course I haven't diverted from to this day. I am grateful for this support and the support I received from close friends and family that echoed these same thoughts in my early years.

I am hoping to now be one of those same voices for others. We only get so much time on this planet and I think it would be an absolute shame to do anything other than pursuing what makes you happy at home, work, and play.

Dedicated to my mother Linda, for always telling me to do what makes me happy.

Dedicated to my wife Michelle, for showing me what it means to be truly happy.

Dedicated to my daughters Belle and Maeve, may you always pursue what makes you happy.

Dedicated to every person who was told they shouldn't pursue a career as an actor.

INDEX

Section One   **Words of Advice**

1. The rule of three   1
2. Is acting a craft, or is it art?   2
3. The power of "No"   3
4. Set your value or others will set it for you   4
5. Be better than you were yesterday   5
6. Serve the story   6
7. Live with gratitude, not expectations   7
8. Learn how to effectively measure success   8
9. The best part of your audition   9
10. Focus on the toolbelt, not the resume   10
11. You are a mirror   11
12. It's okay to   12
13. Avoid comparing yourself to others   13
14. Do not just say "Yes"   14
15. Do not judge your characters   15
16. Acting is not therapy   16
17. Failure is an illusion   17
18. Being over-prepared   18
19. Fear to excitement   19
20. Happiness is a choice   20
21. Be relentless   21
22. What's yours is hours   22
23. You are what you think   23
24. This means more to me right now   24
25. Find the fun   25
26. What's not on the page   26
27. If it is written, it is so   27
28. Why not you?   28
29. Fall in love   29
30. Become a nun's fashion designer   30
31. Be kind   31
32. Ask questions   32

INDEX

Section One   **Words of Advice**

33. Be authentic — 33
34. Get those cows up the mountain — 34
35. Be a firefighter who can act — 35
36. You can't do what you don't know — 36
37. The early bird gets the role — 37
38. Watch TV, see plays, go to the movies — 38
39. Don't seek suffering, it will find — 39
40. Be a colleague, not a fan — 40
41. We ride together, we die together — 41
42. The social club — 42
43. The audition is the job — 43
44. No shame in your game — 44
45. Respect the space — 45
46. Mugshot & rap sheet — 46
47. You be you — 47
48. There is no spoon — 48
49. It's all subjective — 49
50. Just do the work — 50

Section Two   **Preparing Your Audition**

1. The G.R.E.A.T. O.P.E.R.A. — 51
2. Goals — 55
3. Result — 57
4. Emotion — 59
5. Assertion — 61
6. Tactics — 63
7. Obstacles — 65
8. Personalization — 67
9. Environment — 69
10. Relationships — 71
11. Age (or Time) — 73

INDEX

Section Three   **Audition Preparation Example & Worksheet**

1. Sample breakdown on sides   74
2. Sample blocking your audition for camera   75
3. Audition prep worksheet   76

Section Four   **Audition and On-Set Exercises**

1. Square breathing   78
2. Presence   79
3. Connection   80
4. Truth in fives   81
5. Hey DJ   82
6. Role reversal   83
7. Essence   84
8. Repeat the goal   85

BONUS:

Section Five   **Headshots, Demo Reels, Resumes, & Agents**

1. Headshots   87
2. Resumes   89
3. Demo reels   94
4. Voice-Over demos   96
5. The 8 tones of selling   99
6. Agents   101
7. Glossary   103
8. Actions you can do to people   104
9. Story Institute   107

THE RULE OF THREE

I have a personal philosophy I use when deciding on whether or not I want to work on a project. My philosophy is the rule of three. In order for me to be interested in a project I need two out of the following three categories to be interesting or worth pursuing. Anything less than two? I do not pursue the opportunity.

The script.

The people.

The compensation.

Ideally, every project will involve amazing people, a brilliant script, and compensation that keeps us financially satisfied for our efforts and contributions. You only ever need a combination of any two of these to put a project into consideration. Anything less than two? I do not pursue the opportunity.

Great money? But bad script and people you probably wouldn't want to work with professionally? Not interested.

Great script? Great people? No money? I'm in.

If a project has two or more of the three things considered imperative, according to the rule of three, place this project in the "interested" pile.

In the early stages of our careers, it is important to get as much "stage time" as possible, but don't do it at any and all costs, and don't do it just because you are flattered someone asked. As actors we often face more rejection than seems fathomable and when someone is interested in us it becomes extremely compelling.

Stick to the rule of three. You'll work happier and with a greater sense of purpose.

 1

IS ACTING A CRAFT OR IS IT ART?

The word "art" is often used when referring to works that express feelings, emotions, and vision. The word "craft" is often used when referring to a set of learned skills and techniques. Art serves an aesthetic purpose, where craft serves a decorative or functional purpose. So what is acting? Is it an art or a craft?

"Art" is often connected more closely with raw talent, while "craft" often suggests anyone in the world, can learn any skill, if they are willing to work hard enough.

Why can't we do both?

This is a learned skill we continue to develop over time that also serves to express feelings, emotions, and a vision for how the world was, is, and could be. The work of an actor is the perfect hybrid of these two ideas, art and craft.

For those wishing to make this career choice something that brings in a fiscal return so you can pay for food, rent, and other nice things—

Never let one of these ideas trump the other.

Never rely exclusively on your art or your craft if you want to find true happiness in your work. Pursue both relentlessly, and don't settle for anything less than both.

THE POWER OF "NO"

It is no secret. The life of an actor can be a life of feast or famine. We are often programmed to take any audition or role offered to us, partly in fear of not being asked again if we refuse. This is more prevalent in our earlier years as professional actors where we are actively building our resumes, trying to showcase our skills and diversity, and just grateful for any opportunity to work alongside other creative individuals on a similar career path as our own.

But here is where it is important to realize you can always say "no." I am not just referring to the types of roles you will perform or the lengths you will got to for your craft. I mean this also in the most general sense of word.

I still remember the empowerment I experienced when I turned down an audition for a role I had been requested for in the earlier days of my career. My agent was blown away that I would have the audacity to turn down an invitation for a role in which I has been specifically requested. While these are never a guarantee of work, it is often a sign that your odds of booking the role are increased exponentially.

But the audition was scheduled for the same day I was leaving for my honeymoon. I had discussed the opportunity in advance with my wife, and she said she would be fine either way, and I believed her. She is an incredibly kind and supportive soul and delaying our departure by a day or a few days likely wouldn't be the end of the world. But I decided early on that I would have work/life balance, and as important as my career was to me, my personal life must also be equally important. This is one of those moments where I chose to keep my commitments and pass on the acting opportunity.

The role ended up going to a friend of mine who made a lot of money on this show for years, and yet I have never looked back with regret. It wasn't my first audition and wouldn't have been my last. I don't turn down a lot of opportunities like this one, but I am very happy I did on that day and kept my promise to my wife and maintained the idea that our marriage would always come before my career.

SET YOUR VALUE OR OTHERS WILL SET IT FOR YOU

You always have the ability to set your worth. In fact, if you don't, you leave the door wide open for someone else to set it for you and chances are you will have it set far lower than you would ever set it.

This is a career where you can be offered all kinds of compensation from food and a copy of your work, to more money than you could spend in a lifetime.

However, you must be prepared for others to not see your value and risk them pursuing someone else they can hire at a better rate or deal. It is imperative for the professional actor to set their own value. This can be "scale" (what we call "minimum wage" in the acting industry) or it can be above scale or below scale. But you always have the power to decide.

Be realistic, but never apologetic for asking for fair compensation for the skills and experience you build over your career.

BE BETTER THAN YOU WERE YESTERDAY

The greatest gift of acting can also be seen as one of the greatest frustrations. You can ever perfect acting. There is always more to learn. There are always new layers of yourself and the craft to explore and reveal.

Arthur Ashe Jr. once said, "Success is a journey, not a destination."

This is undeniably true about the pursuit of being a professional actor. There is never a magical day where you "just get it" or receive validation or a credential that clearly defines you as successful. Actors should never seek to perfect the craft or learn enough so they can stop learning and start doing. We learn and we do in a never ending, perpetual state for our entire careers.

Don't worry about making it or when you can use the phrase "professional actor" when describing what you do. Only worry about being better today than you were yesterday.

You will find a parallel mindset with athletes who achieve high levels of physical conditioning. There is never one workout where all the muscles pop up out of nowhere. It is always the result of consistent, dedicated work.

Have you completed a tiring or extreme workout only to look in the mirror to see no change? Acting is the same thing. If you want elite level results, you need to consistently work hard, and for extended lengths of time. If you do this, incredible results are inevitable. And not unlike our physical fitness friends, if we choose to stop "working out" we inevitably lose the results we've acquired.

SERVE THE STORY

Be careful not to learn just your lines, or the events of a scene only from your character's perspective. A story is about numerous characters and ideas and each one of them has a specific role in the thematic premise of the story being told.

An actor has one job.

It is not to simply learn your lines.

It is not to try to behave with authentic emotions.

It is not to make people feel.

It is not to become the character.

While your job may include many, or all, of the things listed above, an actor has only one job…

Serve the story.

How does your character contribute to the thematic premise in each scene and throughout the entire script?

Before learning your lines or finding a personalization to create authentic emotions, you first need to determine how your character serves the story.

LIVE IN GRATITUDE NOT WITH EXPECTATIONS

One of the greatest lessons I've learned in my life extends far beyond the walls of my acting career. This change in mindset and attitude has allowed me to find greater joy and peace in all that I do. And while this is an incredibly easy concept to understand, it takes real effort and time to effectively apply it to your life.

Having our expectations unfulfilled or not met is one of the most infuriating things in the world. Walking into any situation with expectations is a sure-fire way to set yourself up for disappointment at some level, whether these expectations were on yourself, someone else, or the universe itself.

When going into an audition, try replacing your expectations of nailing the audition to simply being grateful for the opportunity to read for the role. Trust me, this is way easier said then done and I know I lied to myself often during the first times I tried to convince myself I was replacing expectations with gratitude.

Trying to control our experiences or fighting for perfection are battles that can not be won and they will disappoint you most of the time.

You are a professional actor. You get to pursue your craft and your passion as your career. Maybe not exclusively right now, but you are on a path where this is a possibility. Be grateful. Enjoy the moments. These moments are the ones we will treasure most.

LEARN HOW TO EFFECTIVELY MEASURE SUCCESS

The most common response to "How did the audition go?" I hear after an actor auditions falls into one of two answers:

"It went awful. I totally missed a line"

or

"Nailed it. I didn't miss a single line."

While memorizing the lines is respectful and a part of the job as a professional actor, this should never be your measuring stick for success. Don't get me wrong, learning your lines is important, but it's not the thing that determines the success of an audition. They aren't looking for amazing line rememberers. They want to see what the character looks like and sounds like from you and how the story is served with you in the role.

Try not to measure success by whether or not you book the role. This is something that we can't control and has too many subjective variables.

Use a different measuring stick for determining the success or failure of your auditions.

Measure the results of your auditions by the following:

(1) Did I do what I meant to do? (Did I do what I prepared?)

(2) Was I able to take direction? (If applicable.)

(3) Did I do enough preparation to understand how this character serves the story?

If you do the three things above, consider your audition a 100% success.

If you do this 100% of the time, you will find you will book work. Not 100% of the time, but if you prepare like you will book 100% of the time, you will book consistently.

THE BEST PART OF YOUR AUDITION

Never let your wardrobe or your props be the best part of your audition.

Is it okay to bring in props?

If I am auditioning for a doctor should I wear hospital scrubs?

Can I bring in a toy gun that looks real?

Every casting director will have different rules and preferences. Some will be okay with one thing and not another and another casting director may have a completely different opinion. My golden rule for props and wardrobe is simple—

Don't let your wardrobe or props be the best or most memorable part of your audition.

You are not shooting the actual movie or TV show, so they don't need you to do the work of the professional props or wardrobe departments. I have often used the rule of "What would this person wear on their day off?" as a guideline for wardrobe, and when it comes to props, I try to keep it to the following items, if any at all—

- Cell Phone
- Pen
- Water Bottle
- Clip Board
- Tote Bag

They don't want to see if you can provide props or wardrobe. They want to see you walk in, let's say for a firefighter role, and think "Yup. That looks like a firefighter!" If the only way we see you as a firefighter is when you're in the full gear, carrying a big axe and lugging around a giant hose? You're probably not right for this role.

FOCUS ON THE TOOLBELT NOT THE RESUME

Actors looking for a competitive edge over others will often look for "resume builders". They will take a month with a coach recognized as a top coach, they may even take a casting director workshop so they can add those names to their resume, they may take a weekend special skills workshop to create the illusion of a diversified skill set. While many of these teachers are amazing in what they do, if you don't give them an opportunity to give you a new skill set you are throwing money away for the ability to say you've met these people. There is an enormous difference in working with an acting coach for four weeks and committing to several months.

My advice? Don't take a class or a workshop just to add it to your resume. Worry less about what names and training a on your resume and focus entirely on what skills you can add to your toolbelt. Training once a week for four weeks is often available, but this is almost never enough time for you to learn a skill that you can apply to your craft. You may be able to understand what the skill is, but you can't consider it a tool for your toolbelt until it is something you can routinely apply with little thought and without hesitation.

YOU ARE A MIRROR

Being an actor is a unique opportunity to be a reflection of how your moment in time sees yesterday, today, and tomorrow.

We are a reflection for today's world and the stories we tell offer a deeper look into who we are as a society, who we've been, and who we may become.

My favorite stories aren't the ones that tell me <u>what</u> to think, they are the stories that simply remind me to think.

I love stories that include or end with more questions than answers.

There was a television series, House, starring one of my all-time favorite actors, Hugh Laurie, where this occurred in an incredible way at the end of each episode. They would often tackle complex ideas or moral dilemmas and then not end the episode with the "right" answer, but instead would leave it up to the viewers to reflect on what they had just experienced and decide for themselves.

IT'S OKAY TO QUIT

I quit often. This is a tough industry and sometimes I crave a life without so much rejection, a life without as many authentic feelings spilling everywhere, a life without as much self-assessment. I have an inner brat too. And sometimes he can be very convincing.

But what I have found in my thirty plus years as a professional actor is that I can never quit for long. I am always pulled back into the industry I have grown to know as my calling. Not unlike the "thug life", the actor life isn't something you always choose. Often, the actor's life chooses you.

It's okay to quit. If this is the life you are meant to live? You will never quit for very long.

AVOID COMPARING YOURSELF TO OTHERS

One way to ensure you drive yourself mad is to spend energy focusing on what your other actor friends are auditioning for and/or booking. It will often feel like everyone else is auditioning more than you, seeing more casting directors than you, getting more attention from their agent than you…

And these actor friends will often be in your own category.. They may look like you. They may have similar resumes as you. They will often have similar training as you.

So why them and not you?

Stop it.

This isn't a competition between you and others. This isn't about you versus anyone but you. Focus on being the best you that you can be. Focus on learning more about your craft today than you knew yesterday. Don't work for praise. Don't work for rewards. Work for the understanding of the craft at a deeper level. Work for an opportunity for more authentic self-assessment and self-awareness.

This isn't a competition between you and anyone else.

This isn't a competition between you and yourself.

As a matter of fact, this isn't a competition at all.

This is your craft. This is your art.

Popcorn is prepared in the same pot, the same heat, the same oil, and yet the kernels all pop at different times. Don't worry about the other kernels. Your time to pop will come! Just stay in the pot and stay focused!

DO NOT JUST SAY "YES!"

It is not uncommon for an actor to receive direction in the audition room after their first delivery of the scene(s). This can happen for a variety of reasons . There may be notes from the director, producers, or studio for a specific take or element they want to see in your performance, or they may want to see what kind of range you have with the choices you've made, or they may just want to see it another way for the sake of seeing it another way. It can be anything.

Our initial instincts are often along the lines of:

"OH NO! They hated it. I made the wrong choices! They hate me. I should've done it differently. WHY OH WHY do I make such horrible choices?"

But let's stop to think about this for a second.

If they really didn't like you or if they thought you were incapable of performing the role, would they really invest MORE time in you? Would they stretch out this charade even longer? Just to torment you? To torment themselves?

So now that we've got that out of the way...

Don't just nod and say "yes." I know you're trying to be likeable and directable and all the other wonderful qualities we believe are paramount in being an actor they want to cast and work with time and time again.

Make sure you not only hear the note, but ensure you are able to apply the changes effectively. If there is anything that isn't abundantly clear, ask questions.

A sure-fire way to guarantee you understand the notes or redirection is to say it back in your own words for clarity sake.

So, what I am saying is that you should say "yes" to any redirections, but don't **just** say "yes." Make sure you can apply the "yes" to your performance. Nice people who agree with us are lovely, but people who can apply the note, get hired.

DO NOT JUDGE YOUR CHARACTERS

Ask any actor who has been in this business for any length of time—

What is more fun? Playing good guys or bad guys?

Bad guys will be the response almost every time.

It is important to remember that these characters are fun as they let us access, often forbidden, parts of who we are and say and do things we'd never do in real life.

But these characters aren't different than "the good guys" in how they see themselves, and thus you must honor this when portraying them and their goals with a level of truth and sincerity. Bad guys don't walk around thinking they are bad guys. In fact, they often think they are the good guys.

It is always okay to turn down roles or projects for any reason, but when you accept a role, you have one job - serve the story.

And you must do so truthfully.

Darth Vader didn't walk around thinking "I am so awful. I can't wait to do more awful things to good people who deserve better."

From his paradigm, he was doing the right thing. He was justified.

You can't just try to understand your character, you must become your character and you must always do so from a place of authenticity.

ACTING IS NOT THERAPY

While it often may feel like it, due to the levels of self-assessment and self-exploration we do in our craft, it is dangerous to treat this like therapy.

Actors and acting coaches are not trained therapists, and in my opinion, each of us should stay in our own lanes.

Actors often need to learn to go to dark or vulnerable places and it is imperative that we learn how to come back from these places quickly and safely once a performance is over. Therefore many actors and acting coaches do go to therapists. What we do isn't always easy. I have been in and out of therapy my entire life. I have found it invaluable on a personal and on a professional level. I have also been in it long enough to understand I am not trained to walk anyone else through their own life with any confidence or safety. Not unlike actors and coaches, the therapist's job is complex, difficult, and not something anyone can do effectively without extensive training.

Many actors still believe sad scenes or crying scenes are harder than others. I personally do not subscribe to that theory. It's all hard, and all in the same way.

Whether we are mad, glad, sad, or scared, our job is simple. Serve the story and behave truthfully under the circumstances we've convinced ourselves are real. All of our emotions are fascinating in their own right and none more difficult to access than the other.

Some scenes do require us to go to places that may have connections to traumatic experiences or darker places and having the ability to come out of them in a safe and healthy way is crucial to your own well-being. And it is never a bad idea to spend some time in some form of licensed therapy to ensure you are always taking care of yourself. But don't go to your art or your coach for therapy. We have different roles in your life, and this isn't what we're trained to do.

FAILURE IS AN ILLUSION

Failure is only real if you decide to quit after falling. I am sure you've heard this a million times, from a million different people, but we truthfully do learn more from our falling down than we do from our successes.

In fact, Tony Robbins has gone so far as to say there is no such thing as success or failure, only results. I believe this to be true with all of my heart.

Fall down. Just get back up again. Fall down often. Take chances. Try things you know you can't do. Try them repeatedly until you can do them. This is the actual secret to success that so many people have a hard time identifying. Habits are built from repeating something repeatedly until you reach or exceed the goals you've set. Set habits. Set them by falling, learning from the fall, and getting a little bit better every time you get up again.

Failure is impossible, if you refuse to quit.

Your success is inevitable if you refuse to fail.

Be aware of stasis. The inability or refusal to grow. If your career is suddenly stuck or stagnant, this may not be a reflection of failure so much as a self-imposed purgatory.

It's not enough to just not quit when you fall. You must get up again and try again. If you are not where you want to be in your career, you need to keep training, you need to keep finding new levels.

And when you are where you want to be in your career, you still need to keep training, you still need to keep finding new levels.

In the wonderful words of Arthur Ashe Jr. "Success is a journey, not a destination." And thus we must always be getting up again and be fearless when it comes to falling if we want to see continued growth and success.

BEING OVER-PREPARED

This fees like something exclusive to the actor who focuses entirely on film and television, without any experience or training on stage.

I've heard things like "I only want to look at my audition so I know it, but I don't want to know it so well that I am over-prepared," or "I want to keep it fresh for the audition and have it be really organic, so I don't want to over-prepare."

I do not believe this is a thing.

Keeping a prepared scene or scenes sounding as though you are experiencing live for the first time regardless of how long you've prepared, or how many times you've shot the scene, or how many times you've performed them on stage is the job.

This is one of the very important skills you need to build and be able to access 24/7 for this career. Regardless of how many times you've said your lines or performed this scene, it always needs to sound fresh and present.

So don't worry about "over-preparation" as it is not a thing.

Learn this story. Learn the scene(s). Learn the lines. Learn it all. Learn it forwards and backwards. Learn it so you know it better than the lyrics to your favorite song.

You can't serve the story if you don't know the story. And you can't know the story if you only ever learn it at a surface level.

Will it sound fresh or as though you are saying the words for the first time if you prepare a scene with this level of time and effort? You bet it will. Because this is your job. Regardless of how many times you've said these words, a trained actor will always sound like they are saying them for the first time, every time.

FEAR TO EXCITEMENT

You are nervous and/or afraid because you are about to share something personal and it means a lot to you. Congratulations. Hopefully, every character you play shares this important element of stakes you yourself embody as the actor too.

It is a natural response to what we do, and you will often hear of actors who've achieved great levels of success and those who have been performing for decades say the exact same thing– "I still get nervous before every performance."

These are feelings you don't want to ever lose. But you do want to shift these feelings into their sister feeling… excitement.

Fear and excitement share many of the same physical symptoms:

- Heart racing?
- Sweaty hands?
- Butterflies in your stomach?

Try this exercise. Connect to that feeling. Likely in your stomach. This is where the anxiety or fear likely lives. Now imagine moving these feelings up a few inches into your chest. Do you feel the difference? Transition this energy, don't try to eliminate it.

Move it to a place of excitement and away from a place of fear.

You just turned one of your liabilities into one of your greatest assets.

It gets easier with practice.

Never try to kill this feeling. It is fuel for a much bigger feeling that you can use to your advantage in the audition room, on set, and everywhere else in life.

HAPPINESS IS A CHOICE

Contrary to what the present-day world may tell you, nobody can make you feel anything. Only you can make you feel. Your feelings and how you receive and respond to information is always entirely yours.

My advice? Read Man's Search for Meaning, a book by Victor Frankl chronicling his experiences as a prisoner in a Nazi concentration camp during World War II. In this book he describes his psychotherapeutic method, where he identifies finding a purpose in life to feel positive about and then immerse yourself in it, imagining that outcome. This is an incredible book that every person should read in my humble opinion. Whenever I think I've had a bad day, I'll reflect on Victor's book and what he was able to get through. My problems always feel more manageable afterwards.

You will inevitably face more rejection in this career than most people can even fathom. Think of how many times your non-actor friends go "job hunting" versus how many times you go job hunting. Could you imagine any other career where you hear that many "No" replies where you would still pursue it daily? I can't think of many.

But the happiness doesn't need to live or die with your bookings or what you are being seen for right now. You are pursuing a career as a professional actor. You are often auditioning to work opposite some of your favorite actors. You are a professional actor. This is how you spend your days. As a reflection of society and how we are perceiving this moment in time. This is incredible!

Not unlike professional athletes, you are in a unique group of people who get to pursue their passion as their career. There are hundreds of thousands of amateur actors. But only a few of us have the calling to pursue the craft at the highest level. Congratulations. This is where you are and what you are doing.

This is an enormous accomplishment. And the bookings will come. And the stories you will tell will be amazing I am sure. So choose happiness. It's always your choice. So choose the feeling that brings you joy.

BE RELENTLESS

This is a unique industry and you will have more than enough people telling you to really focus on your plan "B" or to do something else or assuring you that you'll never have any real success in this area or that area.

Some of this will come from people projecting their own fears or regrets or not pursuing their own goals on you. Most of it will come from a good place but an uninformed place, and some of it will just be people trying to validate their own lack of success in certain areas of the business.

Push through it all. Don't just think you can, know you can. And don't just do it with blind faith and determination. Do it with a plan. Do it with a commitment to truly be measurably better every day than you were the day before.

It's easy to quit. And you will see many people you start out with in this industry do so along the way as you continue to grow. A large part of success comes from getting better every day, and another big factor is simply never getting off the train. Don't stop. Despite your own inner brat trying to convince you that you'll never make it.

Be relentless. Keep going. Don't let anyone, including yourself, stop you.

Those who are relentless and commit fully to consistent, measurable growth, inevitably find the path they are seeking. Be one of those people. No shortcuts. No obstacle too big. Be relentless. Make it impossible for you to do anything else.

WHAT'S YOURS IS HOURS

Think about this for a moment. Really think about it. Most people with a 40 hour a week job spend their days as follows—

8 hours a day at their job.
8 hours a day sleeping.
2 hours a day preparing and traveling to and from their job.
2 hours a day eating.

This is 20 out of 24 hours. Every day. This is 83% of your life.

You better love what you're doing if this is how you're going to spend your life doing it. Do you know anyone who works in a job they hate, or don't love? Most of us know lots of people who live like this and it is just considered a normal way of living your life.

Weekends offer you a little more time, but they are often required as catch up moments from the busy work week you've had.

And this is often through your best years! You have a little money in your pockets. You are free to travel. You are free to fall in love. You are free to create the person you will be known as for most of your days. Which person do you want to be?

I don't want to retire. I know lots of people who can't wait to be 65 so they can finally start living. This is insane to me. These people are willing to rush through 40 or 50 years so they can finally enjoy life. I never want to retire. My job isn't something I do in order to survive, it's what I do to truly live. I never want to stop.

You only get so many hours and so many days in this life. Use them well.

Live your best life.

YOU ARE WHAT YOU THINK

One of my favorite movies of all time is the movie "Rocky" by Sylvester Stallone. This is for many reasons, from the script, to the music, to the time in my life when I first saw it... but probably the biggest attraction I have developed for this film is due to its thematic premise. The core message of the film is a universal theme, applicable to everyone in every walk of life.

Think like a loser, and you will be a loser. Think like a winner, and you will be winner.

Overcoming our own inner brat in our own mind is one of the hardest things we can ever do. It's easier to understand the concept than it is to apply it. It's hard. Really hard. But it is what we must do.

Part of the strategy, not unlike what we see in Rocky, is to shift your definition of winner and loser from results to process. Rocky doesn't start training and thinking like a winner after he beats Apollo Creed. He can beat Apollo Creed because he was first willing to do the work and train like a winner and think like a winner. The same will be true in your career. You will likely train harder and longer than you originally thought necessary if you want to reach or exceed your goals. And you will likely feel like you are ready to receive the rewards and benefits from your efforts long before you see them.

This is the secret to success. Be successful in what you do everyday, without looking for overall objectives or final destinations as validation for your efforts or levels of success.

You are what you think.

So what kind of actor do you want to be?

Think about being that person right now. Not eventually. Not tomorrow. Right now.

Start behaving like that person and start doing what they would do every single day.

THIS MEANS MORE TO ME RIGHT NOW

This is an incredibly powerful phrase every actor should not only know but use daily. Nobody is keeping any of the secrets of success away from us. In fact, most of us, actors and non actors alike, are inundated with reminders and opportunities to succeed daily, but we choose to make other things more important at the time and thus we do not see the results we desire.

The best parallel to articulate this point is in the gym membership world. Every Christmas to New year's Eve countless people become motivated to join a gym and lose a few pounds or to get into better shape. They see a bunch of ads on TV and it sounds so easy, because it can be, all you must do is choose to eat right every day and get in 30 minutes of exercise 3-5 days a week. Sooooo easy. And gyms are often selling memberships for such reduced rates, everyone feels inclined to make the changes needed!

And then January 2nd happens, and you'd like to go but you must do this thing, so tomorrow! Definitely tomorrow. And you'd start eating right, but since the gym starts tomorrow, why not start the eating tomorrow too? And this goes on and on until the following December. That's when you realize, THIS YEAR is the year I'll do it.

Actors do the same thing. What are a few simple things you could do for even 30 minutes a day that would have an epic change on your career?

Eating right? Proper meal prep?
Working out?
Acing class?

Could you give up 50% of your tv time and/or social media time? Is this 30 minutes a day? Statistically you would probably have at least 2 hours if you gave up 50% of this time every day. When it comes to things like sleep, food, shelter, we don't prioritize these below anything else. We eat every day. We sleep every day. We have a roof over our head every day. No excuses. Nothing comes up to change this. But how often have you delayed the gym? Or how often have you not skipped your acting class or missed an acting class for something else? You get to decide what's important. You get to choose what you can miss and what is simply unmissable. Choose wisely.

FIND THE FUN

In my experience there are two very different opportunities when it comes to "finding the fun" that may allow you to find interesting choices, motivations, or responses to offers you receive.

(1) Finding the fun as the actor.

Ask any actor what they prefer to play, good characters or bad characters, and I guarantee 99% or more will say "bad guys for sure!" This is often because it allows us to explore a forbidden side to our personality that we don't reveal in proper society or polite conversations. This doesn't mean we are all evil at heart, but not unlike it was when we were toddlers, it is often fun to explore our cheeky or naughty side, even if only for a moment in a scene. Most good people don't know what it feels like to be bigoted or misogynistic or cruel, but as actors you are sometimes asked to go to this dark place and portray it authentically. "Fun" may not always be the correct word to use here, but it is a rare opportunity to understand your potential for darkness that most traditional jobs never ask you to explore or reveal. It is a part of our basic nature as toddlers to see what we can get away with or what we can do to get a reaction from authority. It's natural. Just don't let it consume you and always remember we turn it on and off with the job, never let it spill into your real world.

(2) Finding the fun as the character.

Many scenes are a situation of power struggle, or a battle for higher status. Some are a game of who is going to say "I love you" first, or who is going to be the first to admit the other person is right. There are numerous "games" or "fun" things you can find for the character in the scene. An example of this in action is when Judd Nelson's character, Bender, mocks Brian's parents in the John Hughes movie, The Breakfast Club. There isn't a right or a wrong here, it is a subjective opportunity and multiple options are often available if you truly mine the text for the deeper meaning or if you take the time to do the preparation (see the G.R.E.A.T. O.P.E.R.A. on page 51) for both characters. Doing the homework for both, or all characters, in a scene often offers a deep aspect to your own character that most actors simply never consider. If your job is to "serve the story" and doing the G.R.E.A.T. O.P.E.R.A. for all characters always helped you do this, I would ask why would you ever do anything else?

WHAT'S NOT ON THE PAGE?

Writers have a finite amount of space on the page. It would be impossible for them to describe everything they are thinking, and it would also create a system of robot actors when it came time to perform the work. Writers usually try to write the most specific version of dialogue and action they can, that can be read in the same amount of time this part of the story would occupy on screen.

Therefore, actors are left with the responsibility, and the opportunity, to find what's not on the page in their performances. Note here the importance of never doing anything that betrays the facts of the scene (see the next page) or doing anything that becomes interesting for the actor and takes them out of being interested and authentic. Finding what's not on the page can be found in anything from how you are responding to the offers being made by other characters, to your own character quirks, to your scene activities (i.e. "business"), to laughing, sighing, snorting, or anything else that might add a distinctive element.

I can not stress enough this can never supersede what's on the page, but the actor who can also combine what's not on the page will often find themselves creating more complete characters and will build a reputation for "making interesting choices."

One of the most common mistakes I have seen in auditions is the actor doing what I'd call a monologue in the middle of a scene. This happens when an actor acts one way during the times they are speaking, but then they appear to stop and wait and stare patiently while the reader is delivering the lines for the other side of the scene. Just because you aren't speaking doesn't mean your goals have changed. It doesn't mean you've stopped using tactics. It doesn't mean anything is different in your motivations compared to when you are speaking.

IF IT IS WRITTEN, IT IS SO

The facts of the scene are indisputable and irrefutable. If it is written, it is so.

This applies to what is given to you in character breakdowns, synopses of the story or scene, the action lines, the dialogue, all of it.

Writers, producers, directors, casting directors, do everything they can to give you the best chance to book the role with their breakdowns and the script itself. Nothing is said by accident or without intent. Read everything you can from the breakdowns to the parts of the script that are crossed out in your scenes as you search for the facts of the scene. Once you have read it all, read it again. When you break down your scene(s) and start creating your character needs to include all the clues you were given, and you can never make a choice that betrays what is written.

Never skip over the FYI section of your audition sides. Never scan the breakdowns or only read information about your character alone. You must want to know everything. When possible, read the entire script. If you are to serve the story, you need to know as much about the story as possible and not over-simplify things to "what are my lines and what are the cue words the other characters say?"

If you truly read everything you are given, you will find more than enough information to build dynamic characters who have a clear role in the story.

WHY NOT YOU?

I often think one of the reasons I've been able to achieve the roles and opportunities I've experienced in my life comes down to not being never smart enough to realize it might not be possible for someone like me with my background to have unlimited success.

I've never looked at any performer and thought "I could never do that" or "I wish I was born there" or "man I wish I looked like that",… I have always blindly assumed that smart and hard work will lead to zero ceilings on my success.

It's not like successful actors before us were born on some far-off planet and received super acting powers when exposed to our yellow sun once they arrived here. They are all people, just like you and me. So why not us?

Does your country of origin on your passport make you less of a person? Does it make you incapable of understanding human behavior at the highest level? Are you not capable of following the exact same steps these other people chose in your pursuit of fulfilling your dreams?

So why not you?

There is no reason to think anyone deserves it more than you do. So go get it.

I haven't even met you and I'd put all my money on the idea that you are likely amazing and capable of whatever you put your mind to in this life.

Somebody has to play amazing roles… *Somebody* has to work smart and hard…

So why not you?

FALL IN LOVE

One of the things I have found, as I grow older, is how magical learning can be.

I still remember being in school, for what felt like forever, wondering when all of this "learning" could be over so I could start "doing." Now, all I want to do is go back to school and learn all day. I guess when they say "the grass is always greener on the other side" they weren't kidding. I feel so strongly about this concept, I wrote and starred in a movie about this very thematic premise. It's called 37-teen, check it out.

So, here's my advice if you want to not only get better at acting but get better every day for the rest of your days– fall in love with learning. Knowledge is power and it can be intoxicating. Don't try to learn just enough to get started or to get by. Learn enough to be hungry to learn more. I love learning. Not just acting either. I love learning anything. I am fascinated with our human potential and what we are capable of doing.

And don't be monogamous with learning. Fall in love with stories. Fall in love with movies. Fall in love with plays. Fall in love with art. Fall in love with human potential. Fall in love with yourself and the journey you are on.

There will never be a magical day where you book THE role or THE show. You are doing it NOW. You are a professional actor. You read for professional gigs and this is what it looks like. Love it all. The good, the bad, and the ugly.

BECOME A NUN'S FASHION DESIGNER

A common denominator in many successful people, is their ability to create successful habits. This isn't to deny your raw talent or any other contributing factor, but at the end of the day, hard work and smart work usually create the greatest rewards. And this is accomplished through creating incredible habits. (Nun's? Habits? Some of these jokes are just for me).

Sure, sometimes people win the lottery and become millionaires, but this is hardly a sound business strategy. Same rules apply here. Could you get lucky? Yes. Could you book something epic without really trying or earning it? Absolutely. It happens. Rarely, but it happens. And when it does, it's often a one-hit wonder scenario.

If you really want to create habits that generate success, find the common habits of people who have the success you seek and make those your habits too.

Stephen R. Covey's book, The 7 Habits of Successful People is an incredible resource to give you the tools to do this very thing.

I still remember being an assistant manager for a sporting goods store in my youth when the owner of the company gave all of us… a book for Christmas. Exciting, right? A bunch of teens and twenty-somethings and we bust are butts for this guy all year long and he buys us a book he read and liked. Little did I know, this book would change my life. I still read it often, several decades later. I too now give it out as a gift to those I wish to see succeed and I make all my students not only read it or listen to the audiobook version but use it as a template for my entire educational programs.

Hard work/Smart work beats talent every time.

BE KIND

This can be a tough journey sometimes.

There will be days where it feels like everyone is winning but you. There will be days where you are rejected for what you are convinced is the role or job of a lifetime. There are days when your coolest gig ever, ends. There will be days where it feels like you are a big phony and don't belong with the real actors.

There will be times where you feel <u>you</u> don't even believe <u>you</u> when you are acting.

Remember that. Say it out loud.

Don't be surprised when it happens. It happens to all of us.

So be kind. To yourself.

If you need a pick me up, give yourself one.

If you're having a bad day, know that likely a good day is coming up next. That's how this all works. That's life.

Remember to continuously invest in self-care. If you need to speak to a professional therapist? Do so. I have for most of my adult life without any shame or regret.

What we do isn't always normal, and we subject ourselves to opinions, rejections, and feedback most professions never have to face. Sure a plumber or a dentist may get the occasional bad review on Yelp, but actors can get unsolicited feedback like nobody's business. Social media isn't helping either.

Remember you are never as good as they say, nor are you ever as bad as they say.

Work hard. Work smart. And be kind to yourself

 31

ASK QUESTIONS

If you don't have all the information you need for an audition don't be afraid to ask questions. One of my favorite experiences in the audition room ever was for a role I didn't book, but the experience was a game-changer.

I was reading for acclaimed director, Christopher Columbus. He has directed some of my all-time favorite films and to share a creative space with him was an honor. I remember the role I was reading for was only in a few scenes and there for comic relief. I had done all the research I could in advance, properly prepared the audition, but still didn't have a key piece of information that would have me play the scene very differently based on the desired result. It was a simple question of "Was this a job I was new at or had I been doing it for years?" Chris kindly smiled and leaned forward and said "Interesting. I hadn't thought of that. Why do you think this matters?" I then explained that if it were my first few weeks on the job, I may play it with a sense of unknowing or innocence, but if I have been doing this for 10 years or so, I'd likely have a more jaded perception of everything. Chris was incredibly kind, smiled and said "I love it! Both could work. Do you think we could see both versions?"

So while I still haven't worked with Christopher Columbus professionally on set, I did get one magical audition opportunity with him where we played with the character and story and it changed my confidence level in asking questions forever.

Now, it should be mentioned you need to avoid asking questions regarding information you have already been given in the breakdowns, sides, or anything that may be readily available online. This will have you coming across as unprepared.

But if you don't have all you need, never be afraid to ask questions. Show us you've done your homework and you can apply direction and making choices on the fly. This can be a huge advantage and skill for you in the audition room and on set.

BE AUTHENTIC

Being authentic is the key to all great performances.

But what this page is dedicated to is being authentic outside of the audition room and on set as well. This is greatly appreciated by those in the industry who are constantly bombarded with actors smelling of desperation, willing to say or do anything to stand out and get their big break.

Let's start with "gifting" around the holidays or when you book a gig. This has become more and more common over the years and can be received with incredible gratitude when authentic and have the reverse affect when done inauthentically.

Agents and Casting Directors are often overwhelmed with gifts of chocolate at Christmas and similar generic gifts around the holidays and bookings. There is nothing wrong with an honest symbol of gratitude to an agent who has fought hard for you for months or years when you book your first big gig, or a Casting Director who has given you chances when others haven't… but what is the right way, or the right gift, to show this appreciation? While there is likely no "right" answer, there is always an authentic answer. I might suggest a nice handwritten letter in a Thank you card with a heartfelt thank you for them believing in you and giving you the chance to be your best self.

Whatever you decide to do, if you do anything at all, just remember to be sincere and authentic. While we often convince ourselves we are doing things like this with best intentions, it is also transparent when you are subconsciously doing it just to book more work or be praised yourself. It is supposed to be a thank *you*, not a thank *me*. Make sure you always know the difference.

GET THOSE COWS UP THE MOUNTAIN!

In every scene you perform, you will be best served, as will the story, if you remember to *raise the stakes*. If you ever find yourself shrugging at your own goal, we as an audience are probably doing the same at your performance. When you get to the G.R.E.A.T. O.P.E.R.A. in this book you will see that every character needs to identify a goal in their scene, or a motivation, and you need to identify what it costs you if you don't get it. Making this cost the highest value is paramount.

For example, you may be in a scene where you and a co-worker are eating lunch together and they are stealing fries from your plate. Your character may be trying to explain why they don't share food off their plate to no avail and the co-worker may continue to eat off your plate not realizing their impact.

So what does this cost you?

If your answer is "a portion of my meal" I might suggest seeking a stronger answer. Is it perhaps a reflection of your co-worker's respect for you? When they eat off your plate even though you've been clear how much you don't like it, is it possibly a sign of disrespect? Or perhaps you are too shy to put your foot down and it confirms your own inability to stand up for yourself and therefore your self-worth? I think it is safe to assume either of these choices have greater stakes than "a portion of my meal."

What if you are rejected by someone you have feelings for in a scene? What did you risk? Was it "the chance for a good date?" Was it "your feelings might get hurt?" or was it maybe "the person you end up marrying when you both realize you are soulmates?" What answer provides the greatest stakes?

Caveat: you can't arbitrarily raise stakes if it betrays the facts of the scene. Know the story and know the relationships. The answer is rarely hidden from the actor.

In the last scenario, what would be more interesting for the story?

(a) Might not date that cool person.

or

(b) May be rejected by my soulmate. (Ouch.)

BE A FIREFIGHTER WHO CAN ACT

The casting process doesn't start when you start performing the scene. It starts as soon as you walk into the room.

If casting is looking for a firefighter role for example, they would prefer to see someone walk in who is clearly a firefighter and think "Wow, I hope that person can act!," as opposed to an actor walk into the room where they have to try and imagine "I wonder if that person could believably put out fires?"

This is an extension on the advice on props and wardrobe.

Be the person they want to see from the second you walk in the room. This isn't suggesting you need to enter in character, but you should exude the qualities and characteristics of the role before you even say hello. If we don't believe you in the role before the audition starts, we are unlikely to believe it after we see your work. There is of course going to be exceptions, but by rule of thumb you should try to be what they are looking for in the way you carry yourself before the scene even begins.

I read for a lot of "funny/best buddy" roles. I therefore often enter the room and I am genuinely funny and authentically exhibit the warmth and friendliness you'd find in any best friend.

When I booked the role of Happy on ABC's Once Upon a Time, I had found out my wife and I were pregnant with our first child on my drive over to the audition. Now they had seen countless people already for this role and I was not at the top of anyone's list at the beginning. I entered the room and I could feel there was some tension or an element of frustration in trying to cast these final roles. When the Executive Producer asked me "So, are you happy?" I responded without missing a beat, and with the world's biggest and most honest smile-- "I just found out my wife and I are pregnant, I dare anyone in this room to prove otherwise!" We all had a good laugh and I knew I had booked the role right then and there. I hadn't auditioned a word, but I was clearly able to convey the heart and soul of what they were looking for here.

YOU CAN'T DO WHAT YOU DON'T KNOW

Too many actors spend their early years suffering unnecessarily and having everything they do revolve around their acting. It's like they have no other life outside of booking and auditioning. They are actors being actory and focused entirely on themselves and their careers. This is boring and it's overdone. Be you. Live life. Find balance.

You can't recreate the human experience, if you don't experience being a human. Have friends outside of acting. Stay informed on world events and social issues. Get a hobby, play sports, volunteer for worthy causes. Be a human being.

See plays, movies, and watch television. Go to acting class and discuss the elements of the craft to the simplest and most complex levels. Be philosophical about what different films or performances offer society. Do all of this and get right into it.

But—

Also, do non-actor things. Have conversations that never have your career come up. Don't feel the need to always mention what you're auditioning for or what famous actor you've met, or what movie you are writing. Let conversations be about other sides of you, or even better, not about you at all. Find out more about your friends who are not actors. What interests them? What are their struggles and realities? This will be infinitely more important and valuable than submersing yourself in actor talk 24/7.

And when you make your first projects, try not to make them about how hard it is to be an actor. I know they say write what you know, but there is a reason these projects often fail at any level as they aren't usually relatable to the people who go to movies or watch television. It is tempting and your stories are likely epic, but if they are unrelatable or self-serving they will often have the opposite of your desired result.

THE EARLY BIRD GETS THE ROLE

Being 15 minutes early is being on-time.

So be on time. Always.

Being an actor and behaving truthfully under imaginary circumstances isn't easy. Delivering authentic emotions and goals using the words and actions someone else has written isn't something you just flip a switch and do. So don't.

You need to arrive early enough to do the following:

1. Find out if there is additional information you are getting at the audition that you need to implement into your audition.
2. Fill out any necessary paperwork for the audition. This can be sign-in sheets, non-disclosure agreements, measurement forms, anything.
3. Potentially say hello to other actors you know who are reading for the same project, or possibly the same role.
4. Ground yourself and connect to the performance you've prepared.

If you go into the actual audition room scattered, because you've only just arrived in the waiting area, there is a very good chance you've already blown it. And if you blow it, the casting director may not instinctively think "I bet it's because they had a lot going on today and couldn't get here until the last minute." it is more likely they lose faith in your ability to deliver a professional audition and you are therefore not able to deliver what would be required on set. Nobody ever sees an audition and thinks "Terrible audition, but I bet with more time and some direction they would be good enough to book this role!"

So be on time. Which means "be early." Be ready to go!

WATCH TV, SEE PLAYS, GO TO THE MOVIES

I know far too many actors who audition for TV but proudly boast they do not watch TV.

I know just as many actors today who haven't seen or performed much theatre, nor do they know the names of the great plays or the great actors who came before us.

Countless actors have performed brilliantly before any of us were even born. Countless plays have been written and have defined a generation or changed history. To not know these isn't just a shame, it is disrespectful and indicative you are not ready to take this career seriously yet.

Go to the movies. See plays. Watch television.

By yourself, with friends, with family.

Sometimes just for escape and entertainment and then other times to learn and philosophize. Your job is simple as an actor; serve the story. So you need to know how stories work. You need to dissect different stories and performances and be able to articulate what you liked and what you didn't like and why.

There is nothing cool about being uninformed.

Know your craft. Respect those who are doing what you yourself want to be doing.

DON'T SEEK SUFFERING, IT WILL FIND YOU

The myth of the starving or tortured artist is over-played and life is tough enough –
Don't seek pain. Trust me, it will find you when it is time.

Sleep. Eat. Hydrate. Relax.

I have never understood the romanticized concept of the starving actor or the suffering
actor. Being young is tough and lots of people start with humble beginnings. Why do
we think we're entitled to be special as actors? I have a good friend who got her PhD in
some kind of astronaut, space biology... She's told me a million times and I still don't
get it. Bottom line? She's smart. Like crazy smart. And she also had humble beginnings
when she went to university. She lived on a modest budget, not unlike most actors do.

Most of my teacher friends are in the same boat. And when they graduated school they
didn't have guaranteed jobs waiting. They were on call and were substitute teachers,
and had day jobs, and a lot of parallels to actors. So let's not overplay how hard it is for
actors. It's hard for everybody.

Sure acting can be hard. But so can life. So don't seek the hardship. It will find you.

So whether you are learning to be a space doctor or an actor, the early stages of life
are likely going to be modest all the same.

Bonus: And now catalogue it. Use it. My wife often gets frustrated with me if we have a
disagreement and I say "Can we pause this for just a second? This is good. I can use
this later."

You will get rejected. Life will throw you curve balls.

So don't try to seek it. In fact, seek happiness. It can be just as useful as a tool for your
toolbelt and infinitely more enjoyable.

BE A COLLEAGUE NOT A FAN

If you want to be an actor who is respected by actors and directors with whom you respect and are inspired by, it is important to function as their colleague and not their fan. Being an actor can be tricky in the beginning. You often get to not only meet, but work with, people you've grown up watching on film or TV, and it is sometimes weird.

I've met and/or worked with many of my childhood heroes, and each experience has been different. Often the people they are in real life has been far more impressive and interesting than the characters I knew them as from TV movies.

If you present yourself as their fan, you will likely establish yourself as their fan and that is where you will remain. A fan.

Don't be their fan, be their co-worker. Be to them, what you'd hope they'd be to you in your scenes and just be another talented and hard-working actor on set. If you do this, you will give yourself a better opportunity to someday be the actor that the next generation gets to make this same tough decision with—

Should I be their fan or their colleague?

You don't need to avoid talking about other projects actors may have worked on if it comes up or even taking the occasional "selfie", but don't make this a fan opportunity to interview you favorite, famous actor.

Bottom line? Be real. Do the work. Enjoy the experience.

If you want to be a serious, dedicated, smart actor, let that be your focus for the day. If you want to be a fan who somehow made it on set and even got some lines to say, that is easy to do too. You get to decide which one you want to be.

WE RIDE TOGETHER, WE DIE TOGETHER

Your reader is your scene partner.

Do not "monologue" at them.

Imbue them with what you need them to be.

I have spent a lot of time on the other side of the camera and I am still amazed at how many actors perform their scenes in an audition like it is a monologue, interrupted periodically by the reader. They literally stop acting when they aren't speaking, and you can see them listening for a verbal cue from the reader, so they know when to start acting again. You have a reader, often another professional actor, because we want to see you act in a scene. We don't want to just see you say things, we want to see you receive offers. We want to see you engage another performer or character.

And since we don't get to pick our readers, you need to develop a system that allows you a chance to imbue them with the qualities you need them to represent, regardless of who is your reader for the audition.

If you are reading a scene with your potential love interest for example, you don't get to pick the gender, age, personality, none of it. The reader is the reader. Now go. Same goes if this person is supposed to be your enemy or your mother or anything.

So how do you make the scene organic? Let's say you are doing a scene with your character's mother. What three words could you use to describe her that could be applied anyone?

Maternal? Generous? Over-bearing? Comforting? Cruel?

Fins three words you think work best, and one of the first things you can do in the audition room, is make eye contact with your reader and imbue them with your three words. They epitomize these three things almost immediately. This way, when your eyes meet in the scene, you are speaking to the qualities you need them to represent in your mother... or my lover... or my enemy... or whatever the scene requires.

THE SOCIAL CLUB

You are a professional actor. And the audition room is filled with people who are going through exactly what you're going through. This can be a somewhat comforting sight and feeling and you may feel compelled to share war stories, gossip, and socialize.

Don't.

There is nothing wrong with quick hellos or "we should grab a coffee afterwards," but this is your job and the shift has already started.

You are here to work.

Ground yourself. Breathe. Focus on the pre-game audition exercises and thoughts you need to be at your best.

Do square breathing (see how to do this later in this book) starting on your drive over to the audition and continue it in the waiting room.

Engage in "the essence exercise" (see how to do this later in this book). You can use this to ensure you are authentically in the right frame of mind and heart.

Then I focus on your goal, your assertion, and your environment.

If someone is chatty and not giving you space, it is perfectly okay to tell them you just need a few moments to prepare, but that you'd love to catch up afterwards. Remember this is your job and you've already clocked in.

If you're leaning, you're cleaning. Get to work!

THE AUDITION IS THE JOB

Once you finish the audition, let it go.

Easier said than done. But it's over. Don't dwell on what might be. That was the performance and you probably nailed it. If they want to see it again, they can book you, bring in some trailers, a crew, pay you, etc.

But for now? The job is over. You don't need feedback. This won't help you get the gig. Casting will never say to your agent "Wow. We were about to cast someone else, but now that you've asked us to summarize your client's performance, we realize we almost made an enormous mistake. The job is theirs!"

You will spend most of your career auditioning. So be good at it.

There is an old saying that goes something like this-- "There are those who can do the job, and those who can do the job interview…" I say, why not be good at both?

As 90% of your job and time spent is auditioning, you should be training in this specific skill in an ongoing class. While you most certainly need to build a reputation as someone who delivers on set, you can't build this reputation without first getting someone to hire you to be on set. And this starts with the audition.

Scene study classes are amazing and offer incredible value, but if you aren't mailing your auditions this may not be your best choice for training at this time. Auditions rarely give you several weeks to work on a scene, opportunities to meet with your scene partner(s) in advance to work things through on your own, extensive character development,… Please do not misinterpret this as a statement against scene study. Scene study can be invaluable. But if you aren't strong in the audition room, you need to get strong here, or you will be one of those actors we all talk about.

"They are amazing actors, and always do incredible work in class, I don't understand why they never book anything!"

NO SHAME IN YOUR GAME

Everyone started out at the beginning.

We've all been there.

Day jobs are expected. Don't make it weird.

In a continued message of "be authentic" just be you. If you are working a serving job or something similar and someone from casting or production or anything industry related comes in, do not hide or feel the need to justify making a paycheck.

We've all been there. We've all done it. There is zero shame needed, and no justifications are ever required.

Take this opportunity to be something other than an actor desperate for work. It will be transparent and may smell of desperation. This is a unique opportunity to know them in a different paradigm and connect with people on a non-actor level. This can be more advantageous than an industry networking event.

RESPECT THE SPACE

I have spent decades in various casting studios, and I am always amazed when actors come in to audition and disrespected the space.

They may help themselves to the casting kitchen or the dishes inside, they sometimes make a mess and leave it for someone else to clean up or create excessive noise as they wait to go in and audition.

This is their professional workspace. You are making an impression when you are there so making the right one is important. Make a respectful impression.

This goes for on-set locations, on-set studios, recording studios, traditional theatres, anywhere that you may be working.

Respect the space. Always clean up after yourself. Don't make noise that negatively affects others ability to do their job. Use appropriate language. Behave in a professional manner.

It is surprising to see how entitled actors can sometimes become when we are on set on in the audition room and feeling like we're on top of the world.

Being respectful goes a long, long way for your brand.

People don't just want to hire talented people; they want to hire people they want to be around. Remember the days are often long and repetitive. Being kind, respectful, and professional goes a long way in making sure people want to work with you again.

MUGSHOT & RAP SHEET

Your "mugshot" (aka your headshot) and your "rap sheet" (aka your resume), aren't always needed for every audition anymore.

But my advice is to always have an up to date one on you just in case. Many people in the industry still prefer the tactile feel of an actual headshot and a resume as opposed to scrolling through pictures and text online.

Make sure both are always current, and your headshot should always look like you do right now. If you shave, change your hair color, or do anything else that drastically changes your appearance from your headshot, you need a new headshot. You don't want to hand over materials that require excuses or explanations.

Same goes for your resume. Make sure it is current, authentic, and hopefully contains information that might be interesting enough to start a conversation.

A Casting Director or Director are rarely so impressed by any one credit that has them turn into a fan wanting to know what it is like, but they may find some reason to bring up the experience and talk to you about it.

We only have so many marketing materials and therefore it is imperative and easy enough to ensure they are always an amazing reflection on who we are as a performer.

YOU BE YOU

"Should I call my agent? My friend(s) who look just like me and have the same basic experience and training I do are all auditioning for this thing and I am not!"

It's okay to ask your agent if you've been submitted, but I'd be surprised if you weren't. Your agent only makes money when you make money, so odds are they are on it. It is also okay to ask your agent to check in with casting to see if they'll watch tape if you can't get an official audition request. But you also need to be okay with not being invited to everything.

Casting does their best to see a wide range of talent for each role and it isn't always easy. Sometimes there may be hundreds of people who are all "the right fit" for a role, and they only have time to see 10 people. This means, not everyone who could theoretically do the role will get an invite to audition.

Frustrating? Sure. But not necessarily your agent's fault or an indication that you are at the bottom of the list. It's just not your turn. Nobody is entitled to be auditioned for everything they want to read for and not everyone gets to read for everything they are right for in this industry.

Do you want to audition more? Do you want to be seen for the roles you want to be seen for? Do you want to be top of your category?

Work smarter. Work harder.

The cream always rises to the top.

If you commit to your craft like nobody else in your category, your auditions will become more frequent and you will get more opportunities. But you can't just train "more" you have to train "smarter."

Don't worry about anyone else and what their opportunities are on any given day. You focus on you. I guarantee someone is likely looking at your opportunities right now with the same confusion and jealousy. If we work hard and smart, we all get a turn.

You be you.

THERE IS NO SPOON

The audition is often like the set up of your close-up. The difference being, when we are on set they move the lights and camera to fit your performance, and in the audition room we move our performance to fit the lights and the camera.

Once you have that understood, you can remove the camera and lights from your mind in the audition room. You'd be expected to do so on set and the rules are the same here. You focus entirely on your scene partner and your environment (using loads of suspended disbelief as you imagine the surroundings).

Once you realize there is no camera, not unlike Neo had to understand there is no spoon in the Matrix movies, you can get down to real work.

On set has as many potential distractions as the audition room, more so in some cases, with dozens of crews, trailers, lights, etc. You are expected to just see the set and the other characters. For some unexplained reason this always seems harder in the audition room, but it is your job. If you are not good at it? Get good at it. This is the job.

IT'S ALL SUBJECTIVE

Everything everyone says, including everything I have and will in this book, is subjective.

There will never be a day when all agents agree "this is how we do _____" or a day when casting directors say "_____ is what we want to see you do in every audition room for every audition." This is a subjective industry and we have one job as actors, serve the story. So don't focus on what you think others want to see or hear and instead spend that energy on learning how to be a better storyteller who can self-assess their ability to deliver authentic and engaged performances. This isn't to say you shouldn't be able to take direction, in fact it is imperative that you do learn how to do this efficiently and effectively, but you need to hang your thoughts on your performance on your own feelings and not the subjective feelings of others. In fact, I suspect you could have three different agents or casting directors see the exact same performance and you would likely get three completely different assessments of what they liked or didn't like. Remember they have a creative role in the process as well and deserve the same opportunity to explore this side of their job too.

When I first started out, I heard all kinds of feedback from agents and casting directors.

"You sound funny. You shouldn't do radio, just cartoons."
I've recorded hundreds of radio ads that didn't need a "funny" voice.

You're short. You'd be a good dwarf or elf.
I've played my fair share of dwarfs, goblins, gringotts, elves, etc., but most of my work has been for regular everyday people and my height hasn't hurt my opportunities at all.

No one person's subjective opinion about your performance, abilities, or opportunities should ever deter you from pursuing your dreams to the fullest and beyond.

Don't take criticism from someone you wouldn't go to for advice.

JUST DO THE WORK

There isn't a secret or universal trick that cheats you up the line.

You want to be respected in this business? You want to stay in it for a long time or possibly your whole life?

Just do the work.

I wish I could give you the right drink or acting class or agent recommendation that would ensure success, but that's not how it works.

While there are no guarantees, I have yet to meet one person in my thirty plus years as a professional actor who didn't have some form of success by working smart and working hard.

You will also find others who are not willing to work smart or work hard will quit and make your competition for roles smaller. They jump off the train because they think it got too hard, and truthfully, they just never understood what kind of actual work was required.

Stay on the train. Just do the work.

You will get your turn, and hopefully many, many more after that!

PREPARING

THE

AUDITION

You've got this!

Butterflies in your stomach. Sweaty palms. Trembling legs. A pounding heart.

These are some of the more common physical symptoms of fear or nervousness.

They are also the identical sensations we experience when we are excited.

When you find yourself getting nervous or afraid, replace the thoughts with the idea of being excited. Say it out loud, "This is exciting!" Don't wait for your next audition, try it everywhere. As often as possible. You can alter negative patterns of thought and even come to embrace these sensations through repetitive, mindful approaches such as the idea being presented here.

Focus on the here and now. Focus on gratitude.

This leads to a second enormous mind shift you can apply in changing these negative thought patterns into empowering ones.

The weight of expectations can be more than anyone can bear. And when it comes to the thought that the next audition could be the one that changes everything can be overwhelming. In a similar approach to how we transition fear into excitement, try changing your expectations into gratitude.

Sanford Meisner once said, "Acting is behaving truthfully under imaginary circumstances," and this is perhaps the most definitive phrasing I've ever heard in terms of describing what actors do on stage or on camera. This book will not be an all-encompassing information resource that will unlock all the secrets of acting. In fact, no book or teacher can deliver anything close to this idea. A commitment to a life as an actor is a commitment to a lifelong pursuit of education and finding new levels. Hopefully, this doesn't scare you, hopefully it excites you.

What this book will however give you, is the ability to walk into any audition room, anytime, and deliver the type of performance that gets you invited back or booked! Nobody books 100% of the roles, but if you deliver a bookable audition 100% of the time, you will find yourself in more audition rooms and booking many more roles.

"SET YOUR OWN VALUE
or someone
else will set your value for you."

Chapter One - The G.R.E.A.T. O.P.E.R.A.

Every character, in every scene, in every story, ever told can use the tools broken down in this section to create a confident performance. These building blocks should not be considered the exhaustive elements you can implement in your audition, but the non-negotiable components you never deliver a performance without.

You have one primary objective as an actor, **_serve the story_**. This means the entire story and not just your specific lines and actions. The first thing many actors do when they first get an audition is **_learn their lines_**. On one hand it is hard to find fault in this instinct as we often receive our audition notices with only a day, or two notice and we are often balancing our other real-world commitments like work and sleep and everything in between. In this same respect, I often hear a lot of actors value the success of an audition by their ability to remember all the lines.

"It was an okay audition, but I forgot one of my lines."

"I managed to get all of the lines right (finally) and I guess we'll just wait and see!"

This is never a line remembering contest. I don't want to be misunderstood in the importance of respecting the lines and honoring the writers work, but this is not the determining factor in whether you are right for the part. Casting Directors and Directors and everyone involved in the process assume you will have the lines down for the day but what we really want to know is do you understand how this character **_serves the story_**?

So what is the first step? I suggest you start by learning the story. Not just your lines, but the story. If you have access to the entire script, read it. All of it. Know how this scene affects the characters overall journeys. Now read the breakdown. Not just for your character but for all of the characters available. If this is a television series, watch an episode or two if you have access. Learn as much as you can about your character's potential paradigm.

Now, read each scene at least three times over before making any choices or commitments. Don't skip the action lines, don't skip through other character's dialogue. Read each line with as much reverence as you would your own character's lines.

And finally, before you start memorizing your lines, go through your GREAT OPERA and figure out how you can best serve this story.

Once you have the GREAT OPERA down? Now. Go learn your lines.

The more you do this entire process from start to finish, the faster you will be, and the stronger your choices will be as well.

"Be *INTERESTED* not *INTERESTING*."

"Pursue your goals **RELENTLESSLY** and with **PURPOSE**."

Chapter Two – GOALS

WHAT DO YOU SPECIFICALLY WANT OR NEED FROM YOUR SCENE PARTNER?

This is sometimes referred to the actor's or character's "objective" or "motivation." It is the driving force that moves your character with purpose from beginning to end. Everything that you will do with the GREAT OPERA will reflect towards this backbone of the entire scene.

When you have access to the entire script you will be able to reveal the character's over-arching goal for the story, and each scene will be a step in the direction of that larger goal. Your goal is something you will find either in the pre-life of the scene or somewhere near the beginning. It was what you specifically want or need from your scene partner, in terms of what you want them to do, feel, or understand.

Remember there is never a right answer in determining your goal. The important factor in identifying the goal is ensuring it aligns with **the facts of the scene**. This is something we will explore deeper in Chapter Fifteen.

An exercise to determine whether your goal works in a scene or not is to try and replace every line your character says with this goal.

For example, "I want you to understand you can't hurt me anymore."

Use this line in place of each of your lines. Does the scene still make sense? If yes, you may have a winner. If not, keep looking for something that fits.

Keep your goals singular. Avoid things like "I want this, because I want that, so I can have this, because I want that…"

Keep it specific. Keep it simple. Your levels of simplicity and specificity will often be directly aligned with your levels of greatness.

Another extremely important aspect of determining the goal is to ask yourself "What does this cost me or what do I lose if I don't achieve this goal?" We often throw around the phrase "life or death consequences" but this doesn't have to mean literal life or death, but it does need to have great importance. The stories we tell are like real life with the boring bits cut out. It has to be important to you or it won't be important to your audience, and this will show in your audition.

Don't feel the need to find one goal. While you need to deliver your audition with one goal, you need to be prepared for a redirect. Exploring multiple options, even subtle ones, can enhance your overall understanding of the story and the role your character plays in it all.

"Be *ENGAGED* not *ENGAGING*."

YES or **NO**. Definitively. There is no room for "maybe", "kind of", "sort of"...

Chapter Three - RESULTS

DID YOU GET WHAT YOU SPECIFICALLY WANTED OR NEEDED FROM YOUR SCENE PARTNER?

One of the most beneficial things I have experienced from working on the other side of the audition camera, as both a reader and as a director, is watching countless actors with a wide range of experiences showcase their craft. I've seen some of the most veteran performers make the simplest of mistakes and I have seen some newer performers make some incredibly effortless and bold choices too.

One of the most common things I experience however, was an alarming number of ambiguous endings. I could often sense the goal the actors had chosen but in numerous cases they ended their scenes without a definitive confirmation on whether they felt their character had achieved their goal or not.

This likely comes from our inherent desire to be liked and to appear versatile, but it comes across as an unfinished scene. I have seen some actors make choices that were one-hundred and eighty degrees opposite of what the Director wanted and come across as much stronger options for the role. This of course came with the ability to apply the redirection, but the key point here is that they were offered a redirection. If you don't commit to a result from your character's point of view it is much harder to offer a redirection.

We should see it in your actions and hear it in your voice. Did you get what you specifically wanted or needed from your scene partner? Make a decision. Often it is right there in the script, but sometimes it is not, but you must always make a choice.

Remember to stay in the moment once you have finished the scene. It is often tempting to feel an incredible amount of relief at the end and to look for approval from the Casting Director or Director. Unfortunately, this will only show you weren't that invested in the scene if you snap out the second you run out of words or actions. Ensure you have a strong moment after. Show them you know this character even when all of the words and actions on the page run out. This doesn't mean extensive adlibbing, but you should be able to stay in the scene completely until the Casting Director or Director calls "Cut!" or "Scene!" This is something we will explore further in Chapter Twelve – Find what's not on the page.

"If you want to be **SUCCESSFUL** in this world,

you have to follow your **PASSION**, and not a paycheck."

~ Jen Welter ~
The NFL's first female coach

Cautiously optimistic

Over the moon excited!

Irate

Worthless

Defeated

Miffed

Destroyed

Homicidal

Terrified

Betrayed

Joyous
Self-Loathing
Resentful
Pleased

Blithe
Startled
Betrayed
Thrilled

Chafed
Vexed
BE SPECIFIC
Aghast

Mournful
Unnerved
Content
Intoxicated

Chapter Four - EMOTION

HOW DO YOU FEEL ABOUT THE RESULT OF YOUR GOAL?

There are 4 basic human emotions—

Mad. Glad. Sad. Afraid.

How did the result of your character's goal make you feel? Be as specific as possible. Does the result make you "happy" or is it more extreme like "euphoric" or perhaps more subdued, like content or satisfied? There is a brilliant book available, written by Marina Calderone, called ACTIONS: The Actors' Thesaurus. This book should be in every actor's audition bag. This book is incredibly helpful here and will be again for all your work in Chapter Six – Tactics.

This is not to suggest you do anything authentic or force an emotion at the end of your scene. This is simply a reminder that the result of achieving or not achieving your goal will likely have a definitive emotional connection and you should be able to identify it in your preparation. The choices made by your reader or other factors during the audition may organically change the degree or specificity of this emotion at the end, but you should be able to identify which of the four basic emotions this will be and to what degree during the preparation process.

It is also important to note that there will be times where you achieve your goal and have a negative response and there may also be times where you do not achieve your goal but have a positive emotional result. This often happens when our characters has a growth moment or realities don't match expectations.

Never play the emotion or force the emotion, always allow it to come authentically. Section Two of this book will offer you different exercises to help you organically connect to all your emotions and call upon them genuinely when needed.

If you commit to your goal, if you imbue the appropriate relationship elements on the reader, if you execute an authentic assertion, if you complete each step of the G.R.E.A.T. O.P.E.R.A. you will find you do not need to reach for your emotions. They will be there for you and completely authentic.

"*USE YOUR SMILE* to *CHANGE THE WORLD*
and never let the world change your smile."

" **I am** _____(character's name)_____..."

"... **and the world is** _____(how do you feel about it right now?)_____

Chapter Five - ASSERTION

WHAT IS YOUR CHARACTER'S CURRENT MOOD OR RELATIONSHIP WITH THE WORLD?

Acting coaches or books will often refer to this part of the process as creating a prolife or a moment before. Remember, acting is real life with the boring bits cut out. The odds that your character *suddenly* discovered their goal for a scene the second it starts on the page is slim to none. Think of your own life. How often do you stew on the drive or walk over? How often do you role play both sides of a conversation in the shower as you try to map out the best way to broach a conversation?

The formula for discovering an appropriate assertion for your character in any scene is simple.

"I am (character's name) and the world is (how your character feels about the world at this moment)."

Not only is this helpful in determining an appropriate tone and direction for your take on a scene, it is also an amazing tactic in making sure you launch into your scenes and don't fall into the common trap of warming up into them half-way through.

In your head, whisper your assertion over and over a moment or two before the scene begins to ensure you are emotionally connected in a truthful and grounded emotional state of mind.

This is one of the few things I recommend focusing on for the audition. Most of the preparation is just that-- *preparation*. If you are thinking about your homework during the scene, you are likely not **committing** to being in the scene.

But this is something useful for many actors to implement just prior to launching into your scene so you are connected and authentic.

"KNOWING YOURSELF is the beginning of all *WISDOM."*

~ Aristotle ~

"TO THINE OWN SELF BE TRUE."

~ William Shakespeare ~

Tactics are **ACTIONS** you do to people.

"I _____ you."

e.g.

Kick	Question	Compliment	Flatter
Tease	Stab	Interrogate	Threaten
Seduce	Challenge	Lecture	Inspire

(More examples on page 104)

Chapter Six - TACTICS

HOW ARE YOU GOING TO ACHIEVE YOUR GOAL?

Not unlike how we behave in real life, our characters have wants and needs throughout the day and the way we pursue these desires or necessities is to use a series of positive or negative tactics in order to accomplish the objective. This is how we navigate or attempt to navigate around the obstacles that try to prevent us from reaching our goals.

These are best described as "actions you can do to people" and the formula to see if the tactic you want to apply works, is to see if your word fits into this sentence– I _____(action verb)_____ you. Based on this formula you can seduce, flatter, interrogate, push, kick, educate, elevate, hug, kiss, inform,… Wait? Hug? Kiss? With words? Yes, you can. Sometimes a warm word can be like offering a comforting hug.

"So what if I want to flirt as my tactic?" I flirt you. Doesn't work, does it? But what are the actions within flirting that you do to people? Flatter? Compliment? Entice? Seduce? See the difference?

One of the greatest challenges of implementing your tactics for the audition or performance is to do so with every expectation of success. You've probably read this scene a hundred times now and know what works and what doesn't work, but your character needs to deliver it like it's an idea they have just come up with on the spot in the now. Why would they try something that doesn't work?

Another common issue is to register what is working and what is not due to the amount of times we review a scene before performing it for others. You need to "Yay" when something is working and "Yuck" when it is not. This doesn't, and shouldn't, be overplayed but we need to see how the result of the tactic lands on you. If something is working, take it further. e.g. If you get close to your goal with a compliment perhaps your next move is seducing? If it doesn't work? Perhaps you need to change directions? Perhaps a failed compliment is followed up with an "I educate you"?

Our tactics are basically our words and our actions. It is what we do to people in the spirit of achieving our goal. What are you doing and what are you saying to make it all happen? This is where the actor's choices comes into effect. Words need to be your friend. Your level of simplicity and specificity are important here. What is the most effective tactic you can perceive for each obstacle? During the early stages of the process try everything, you never know what you may discover as an interesting choice that allows the scene to find new levels.

"A *GOAL* without a *PLAN* is just a wish."

~ Antoine de Saint-Exupéry ~

OBSTACLES can be words, actions, or the environment.

"**Yay**!" and "**Yuck**!" things that are working and things that are not working.

Chapter Seven - OBSTACLES

WHAT IS BEING SAID AND/OR DONE THAT IS GETTING IN THE WAY OF YOUR GOAL?

Every scene has conflict. Every single one. These follow the basic rules of conflict and can be--

Person vs. Person
Person vs. Self
Person vs. Environment

These go hand in hand with the tactics. These are the words, actions, and sometimes environment that specifically prevent your character from achieving their goal.

During the text analysis and G.R.E.A.T. O.P.E.R.A. process I find it best to mark the obstacles and tactics right on the pages of the script.

You don't need to be married to your choices, but you should map them out, so you have a clear understanding of the journey your character is on for each scene. Your scene partner(s) may interpret things a little differently than you and you may find yourself changing tactics on the fly as obstacles are delivered differently than you expected. This is not only okay, it is amazing. It keeps it fresh.

As long as you have prepared a logical thread of obstacles and tactics you should easily be able to go off prep and adjust to whatever is thrown at you.

If the action or words can't be identified specifically as something that is preventing you from achieving your goal, then it is not an obstacle. It may *feel* like an obstacle, but obstacles have a very specific role in every scene. They are the heart and soul of our conflict.

"A lot of people give up just before they make it. You know you never know when ***THE NEXT OBSTACLE*** is going to be ***THE LAST ONE.***"

~ Chuck Norris ~

Does this feel familiar?

Chapter Eight - PERSONALIZATION

WHAT EXPERIENCE HAVE YOU HAD IN YOUR REAL LIFE WITH A SIMILAR GOAL AND STAKES?

This is how you connect with the scene and truly find an authentic understanding of what is involved and what the character is risking or has at stake. To find an effective parallel, you need to identify the essence of the scene and ask yourself if you've had a moment where you felt the same way and had similar stakes. It doesn't need to be identical but as close as possible.

It is difficult to provide an example with proper context unless you have a script or scene to reference, but I will try to do so anyway here—

Imagine your character is up for a promotion at work and is passed over for someone less qualified because they were at the company longer. Perhaps this makes your character feel under-valued and disrespected.

A personalization from your real life may be from a time when your parents overlooked you and gave something to an older sibling that should have been yours. Perhaps it's a hand me down, a cherished family heirloom, that aligns with your personal interests, but Dad gives it to your older sister for no other reason than she's the oldest.

Maybe your character is a mid-level mobster being interrogated by a seasoned detective. The detective is trying to catch you in a lie and to get you to rat out your boss.

Maybe you had an experience from childhood where your parents "interrogated" you after you busted curfew and now, they want you to tell them which friend is responsible for dragging you into this mess?

The key is that it needs to be a real and specific event that you can recall.

If you don't have anything from your history that works you can use what's called an "as if" and imagine what it would be like "as if" someone you knew did something to you. These are generally less effective but something our only option if we don't have a life experience that properly reflects the stakes and elements of the conflict that reflect your actual history.

"Sometimes we're tested not to show our **WEAKNESSES** but to discover our **STRENGTHS**"

"Where are **YOU** and how do you **FEEL** about it?"

Chapter Nine - ENVIRONMENT

WHAT IS AROUND YOU? WHERE ARE YOU? HOW DOES IT AFFECT YOUR SCENE?

What time of day is it? If it's after midnight, are you whispering? If it's a crowded area, are you more protective of your words? Is it hot? Is it cold? Are there people nearby?

If you are in a room with other people, where are they standing? It is often advised to block your scenes with the main person you converse with right beside the camera. Is there a door? Where is it?

There aren't any rules that say you must always look right beside the camera, but most auditions are framed by the camera to resemble what would be your close-up. Thus anything you do that isn't facing the camera is often not captured and effectively didn't happen.

Draw on the back of your scripts and map out where everyone is and any key set pieces.

Try to direct most of your action and dialogue into a pie shape (see below) so the camera can catch it all. There will be times where turning away for a moment is a stronger statement or choice, but it is best to use these sparingly, and always know why you are doing it.

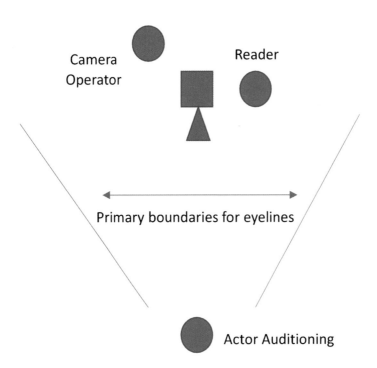

"The key to success is to focus on *GOALS* not *OBSTACLES*"

EVERY scene has conflict.

EVERY scene has a scene partner, even when you are alone.

Always remember the three types of conflict—

Person vs. Person
Person vs. Self
Person vs. Environment

(Sometimes you have more than one of these in the conflict)

Chapter Ten - RELATIONSHIP

WHO IS YOUR SCENE PARTNER AND HOW DO THEY MAKE YOU FEEL? AND WHY?

The temptation for most actors is to describe the relationship with other characters in a scene by what they do for a living (police officer, teacher, doctor,...) or what their biological relationship is (Mom, Dad, Grandma,..) But this hardly describes **who they are to you**. As an experiment find a group of 5 or more people and get them to describe a police officer in one word. You will likely get a mixed assortment of answers from "bully" to "protection" to "corrupt" to "heroes." Now try this experiment with the same people but get them to describe their Mom in one word. Again you will likely get a mixed bag of responses from "loving" to "controlling" to "naïve" to "dinosaur."

The key to this part of the great opera is to reveal **how they make you feel**.

If it's a police officer for example, do they make you feel safe? Scared? Are they a rookie? Seasoned veteran? Are they emotionless? Are they caring? Do they create a feeling of respected authority? Or corruption?

A wonderful exercise to help flush out a relationship is to borrow the "WHY" game from our childhood. Build a character out of WHYs.

E.g. Are they a good cop? Yes. Why? They really love people. Why? They grew up in a rough neighborhood and know what it's like to grow up in tough conditions. Why? Their parents moved here to escape a corrupt government in their home country. Why? They wanted a better life for their children? Why?

Do you see how this can go on forever? Do it as deep as you can and flush out a real person.

Once you have done this, find three words to best describe this character and are something you can imbue upon your reader at the audition. We don't get to pick our readers and they may be a sex, age, height, or any other identifier you aren't expecting, and you need them to quickly embody the core elements of the relationship you've built. Anyone can be intimidating, or caring, or loving, or whatever you design.

Also ask yourself, what is the history? Have you been here before with this person or is this something new? How would you interpret things differently based on something new or ongoing?

"Your **connections** to all things around
you literally define who you are."

~ Aaron D. O'Connell ~

"Our role as artists is to be a reflection of how our moment in time sees
YESTERDAY, TODAY, AND TOMORROW."

Chapter Eleven – AGE/TIME

HOW DOES TIME OR THE TIME IN YOUR LIFE AFFECT THIS SCENE?

There are basically three different types of time in a scene that can determine what choices you make.

Is it morning? Noon? Night? How does that affect your character's energy or state of mind?

Is it past, present, or future? You need this for context. You can not perform a role authentically if you are trying to look at everything through the lens of today. In the movie Big Eyes for example, everything basically happens during the 50 and 60s. This was before the feminist movement of the 70s and women had a very different paradigm with the world. It would be dishonest to play the scene with today's more empowered and liberated eyes. The struggle under the conditions, and the environment of the time is a major factor in the story and an indicator of the strength of the lead character. Often, we portray the future as a more liberated and understanding time, while we view the past as outdated, misogynistic, and ignorant. These absolutely matter in how you authentically deliver your performance.

The other major time piece in every story is the time of your life. In other words, what was the major life event you were going through. In Star Wars: A New Hope, Luke Skywalker is trying to save a Princess and fight off a menacing evil that is taking over the galaxy, during the time in his life where he basically discovers he is "space Jesus" or "the chosen one," and is destined to save everyone.

So what is the time in your character's life? The time you were graduating high school? The time you were getting divorced? The time you met the love of your life?

And how does this affect each scene in the story? In a love story for example, it's common to have a whole series of events relating to the love of your life. The scene where you almost didn't meet the love of your life. The scene where you knew this was the love of your life. The scene where you almost left the love of your life.

The G.R.E.A.T. O.P.E.R.A.

SAMPLE

Page 78

ASSERTION:
I am ADAM and the world is UNFAIR!

EXT. ADAM SMALLS' BUILDING - AFTERNOON

Adam exits Erin's car. She rolls down a window.

Tactic: **I BEG** you.

ADAM
You sure you can't just change the grades?

SPECIFIC WANT/NEED:
Erin to change the grades for all of my classmates.
COSTS ME IF SHE DOESN'T:
Everyone will hate me.

ERIN
Firstly, you'd need every teacher to agree to it and secondly, there's a clause that prevents us from tampering. Eighty percent of the grade is on the final exam for each class.

Obstacle: Not likely to have teachers agree and legal issue.

ADAM
But we haven't taken those yet.

Tactic: **I INFORM** you.

RELATIONSHIP:
I trust her. I respect her. She is authority.

ERIN
Exactly. But everyone quit, so they'll get a zero by default.

Obstacle: Nobody wants to continue

ADAM
But if we all took the test and passed?

Tactic: **I EDUCATE** you.

ERIN
Technically, yes.

Obstacle: It's a tough loophole

PERSONALIZATION:
My second marriage.

ADAM
"Technically"... Wait.

Adam opens a document on his phone labelled "Contract".

AGE:
Present Day. Day time. That time I redid high school at age 37.

ADAM (CONT'D)
This document doesn't state tests can't be "open book", correct?

Tactic: **I PROBE** you.

Erin scans the section he points to on the contract.

From the feature film THIRTY-SEVENTEEN, written and produced by Michael Coleman, distributed by Comedy Dynamics in Burbank, CA.

The G.R.E.A.T. O.P.E.R.A.

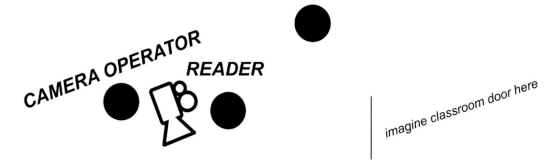

SAMPLE - BLOCKING OF SCENE

imagine a blackboard here

CASTING DIRECTOR

CAMERA OPERATOR   **READER**

imagine classroom door here

imagine empty desks here   **ME**

I will often map this out on the back page of the audition sides.

This configuration of CAMERA OPERATOR, READER, and CASTING DIRECTOR is quite common in most casting rooms.
Sometimes the camera is on the other side of the room or the middle, but this is a common set up.

Audition Worksheet
(Feel free to print this sheet and use if for every scene you audition for or perform!)

GOAL: I specifically want/need my scene partner to (*check only one*) [ ] **do** [ ] **feel** [ ] **understand**

_____

RESULT: Do I achieve this goal? (*check only one*) [ ] **yes** [ ] **no**

EMOTION: How do I feel after I achieve/don't achieve this goal? (*check only one*)
[ ] **Mad** [ ] **Glad** [ ] **Sad** [ ] **Scared** (Be SPECIFIC and don't be afraid to have mixed emotions)

_____

ASSERTION: I am _____ and the world is _____
             (character's name)   (character's state of mind)

TACTICS & OBSTACLES: Mark these directly on the audition or script pages. Circle anything that is said or done that is an obstacle in achieving your goal. Now Mark with a "T" anything that is said or done that is a tactic to get around the obstacle. Be SPECIFIC!

PERSONALIZATION: Identify and recall a specific memory with a similar goal and similar stakes.

_____

ENVIRONMENT: Draw the basic elements on the back of each scene page. (Use the the example on the previous page as a guide) This will help with eyelines and blocking.

RELATIONSHIP: List three words that describe how this character makes you feel

(1) _____ (2) _____ (3) _____

AGE/TIME: What is the time of day? _____

[ ] **Past** [ ] **Present** [ ] **Future**

What is the time of your life? _____

"I believe luck is *PREPARATION* meeting *OPPORTUNITY*.
If you hadn't been prepared when the opportunity came along,
you wouldn't have been *LUCKY*"

~ Oprah Winfrey~

EXERCISES

You likely won't have time for all of these, before every audition or scene on set, and some you may find are more beneficial than others.

These are a series of exercises I have learned from various acting coaches and some are great tools I've "borrowed" from various psychologists, to help me navigate my nerves and prepare myself for an authentic and grounded performances.

Square Breathing

Presence

Connection

Truth in Fives

Five Senses

Hey DJ!

Role Reversal

Essence

Repeat the Goal

The main idea here is to find a way to be present and connected. If you have something that works, continue with this or these techniques.

If you are open to new ideas or searching for something you can make your own, please consider the following as effective tools that can make a real difference.

SQUARE BREATHING

Square breathing, also known as box breathing or four-square breathing, is a technique used to relieve stress, heighten performance and increase confidence.

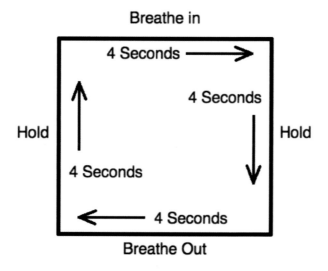

As an actor, we can experience extreme forms of anxiety and stress just prior to auditions or performances. This exercise is an incredible technique that will allow you to ground yourself and be ready for the stresses associate with this job.

It's used by everyone from professional athletes, the military, police officers, and nurses.

I like to use 4 seconds for each of the following steps but there is no reason why you couldn't use 5, or 6, or whatever works best for you.

(1) Breathe in: Slowly inhale through your nose. Try to fill not just the air in your chest but down to your lower lungs as well.
(2) Hold: Fur a slow count of four seconds, calmly hold that breath in.
(3) Breathe Out: Slowly exhale, through your mouth, all the oxygen out of your lungs. Be 100% present as to what you are doing. Focus entirely on the breath.
(4) Hold: For a slow count of four seconds, calmly hold that breath out.

Repeat.

PRESENCE

Close your eyes. Feet at shoulder width apart. Try to still your mind.

Focus on nothing but the now.

Your hands are at your side, out of your pockets, not fidgeting.

Your legs are firm but not locked. Your posture is upright, shoulders back.

Now relax your forehead. Send this thought to your forehead and try to calm this area.

Now send this same thought of relaxation to your jaw. Feel free to open and close your mouth wide and move your jaw around and now let it settle, mouth closed.

Now it is time to release your shoulders. Take a deep breath in and try to lower shoulders on the exhale. Breathe in again, without moving your shoulders up or down, and see if they will go even lower on the next exhale.

Continue sending relaxing thoughts to these three areas of your body, repeatedly. Now send these relaxing signals to other areas of your body. Your calves, your hips, your fingertips, wiggle your toes, and feel the tension leave your body.

As you do this focus only on what is now. What do you hear? What do you feel? What do you smell? What are you experiencing now.

Your mind will want to wander. That's okay, just bring it back whenever it does.

Live in this moment. Live in the now.

CONNECTION

Before this exercise begins, identify one of you as "a" and the other as "b."

This is an extension of the Presence exercise and requires a scene partner. I say it is an extension of the Presence exercise as it is most effective when explored from a place of being completely present and still in body and mind.

Stand a few inches away from your partner, face to face. There can not be any talking or discussion here, you are required to connect without words. You may laugh or even cry throughout this exercise, but you can not speak. Not until it is over.

Implement your square breathing here. Remain grounded, present, and still.

Now "a' will think of a secret they have never shared with anyone. Something incredibly personal. It can be a positive or a negative. Then, "a" will take a few moments to remember as many of the specifics of this secret as possible. Then, without using any words, only their eyes looking directly into "b's" eyes they will share every intimate detail of this secret and every ounce of how they feel about it. This can be emotional, but stay focused, stay connected, stay grounded. Say everything that is in your heart, shouting on the inside if necessary, and get every one of these details out. This should be something very personal and something you would never dare share out loud.

Throughout this entire time, with both of you locking eyes and never looking away, "b" should be saying, with their eyes only, "Thank you for sharing something so personal with me. I respect you unconditionally and I will honor this secret and not share it with anyone else ever."

This can take several minutes and let "a" keep talking, not verbally and only through their eyes, until they feel they have shared everything can say or feel about this secret. Once "a" feels this is complete, they can reach out with their right hand and touch "b's" left elbow to signal it is done. And "b" can do the same with their right hand to "a's" left elbow to reaffirm the gratitude in sharing something so personal.

Now switch roles.

You will likely feel incredibly connected.

TRUTH IN FIVES

This is an exercise I learned in dealing with my PTSD and it has also doubled as an incredible tool in navigating the stress and mind wandering that can occur just before auditions or performances.

The concept is simple enough in nature and incredibly powerful for such a simple idea.

Look around the room and identify 5 truths without thinking.

(1) That chair has four legs.
(2) That wall is beige.
(3) My arm is hairy.
(4) I hear a bird chirping.
(5) The floor is laminate.

It can literally be anything that is simple and true. Repeat this exercise over and over and you will find yourself in place of stillness and truth.

This is also where every performance should be born out of and can be a wonderful starting point just prior to your audition or on set performance.

FIVE SENSES

Since we're revealing PTSD tricks to battle panic attacks, here is another I borrowed from my self-healing that has proven to be magical for auditions and gigs too.

This is similar to the 5 Truths exercise in its simplicity and commitment to being in the present prior to a stressful event like auditioning or performing.

This is all done quickly and without any delay:

Step One: Identify 5 things you can see.

Step Two: Identify 4 things you can feel or touch.

Step Three: Identify 3 things you can hear.

Step Two: Identify 2 things you can smell.

Step One: Identify 1 thing you can taste.
* For this last one it can be whatever you taste in your mouth now, or I like to lick the back of my hand to make it an action item.

This incredible grounding exercise can keep your mind laser-focused on the present and prevent it from bouncing around and letting your anxiety play tricks on you.

HEY DJ!

We all have songs from our youth or history that bring up certain emotions or feelings.

I personally have some interesting ones. I, for example, can not sing the national anthem out loud without crying. I have a conditioned response when I sing it at sporting events that tugs at my heart strings. It has been decades since I have sung this song without bawling. I also have several songs from traumatic events in my life that instantly bring up all the feelings, as though the life-event happened only moments ago. Music can connect us to different time periods, to different life-events, or to just about anything. Music is a powerful amplifier for our emotions and memories.

My advice is to find your songs that are your triggers and build your self an actor's playlist. Have all of them with you on your phone and be able to access them whenever they are needed.

We can, and never should, fake emotions or "try to summon" emotions, but there is no harm in knowing your triggers and having them readily accessible.

ROLE REVERSAL

Do your G.R.E.A.T. O.P.E.R.A. for your character and prepare the role like you would any other. Once you feel like you really have it and you are ready to audition, switch roles and start again.

Perform it out loud with someone. Do it two or three more times out loud.

Now prep the other role like it is the one you are going to be performing.

Do every step as you did for your actual role.

Now do this role out loud. Have your friend/scene partner do your original role out loud. Repeat this a few more times.

Now go back to your original role.

Did you find anything new throughout this process? Do you see the story the same way? Do you have new ideas you want to implement in your G.R.E.A.T. O.P.E.R.A.?

Don't be afraid to adjust your "finished audition prep" if you discover something new through this process. Our work is always a work in progress.

If an actor's only real job is to serve the story, what better way to execute this job than to truly know the story from various paradigms within the scene.

ESSENCE

This is a great way to get to the heart of a scene or story and also doubles as an exercise that can inform your choices for your Assertion in the G.R.E.A.T. O.P.E.R.A.

(1) Essence
(2) Personalize
(3) Fantasize
(4) Reminisce

Essence: If you had to describe the scene in a word or short phrase, what it's truly about, what would it be? Think terms of betrayal? Lost innocence? Unconditional love? Forbidden pleasure? Disappointment? Power struggle?

Personalize: Now ask yourself if you have ever experienced something like this in your real life. Be specific. Something that not only has the same essence as the scene but hopefully similar levels of stakes.

Fantasize: Now imagine what you'd like to say now (or then) if you could speak to that moment. If it is a moment of comfort perhaps you may want to say, "I love you," if it is a moment of disappointment perhaps, you'd want to say "I'll never forgive you." Be as specific as possible with the memory and let yourself be honest with what you'd want to say. Now say it in your head. Over and over. What feeling does this create?

Reminisce: Now that you've done the exploratory work, just focus on repeating the phrase over and over in your mind. Never out loud. And now try to recall whatever else that personal moment was to you in terms of your other senses. What did you hear? Smell? Touch? Anything that makes the memory more vivid.

When done properly, and it does take time to develop this skill, it can help place you in an authentic emotional and mental state that reflects where your character is too if the essence of the scene and your personalization match.

REPEAT THE GOAL

The goal, or the "motivation," or the "objective," is effectively the heart of every scene. Is it what drives each character's words and actions and the opposing goals create the conflict that is necessary in every scene.

So how do you know if your goal is a good choice?

One effective exercise is to replace every piece of dialogue for your character with your specific goal and have your scene partner or reader perform the other characters as written. Let's say for example your goal is "I want you to understand you can't hurt me anymore." Replace all of your lines with this line. Truly hear the offers being made by the other characters in the proper text and respond authentically but using only the word—

"I want you to understand you can't hurt me anymore."

Does the scene still basically work?

If yes, you may have a solid choice here for your goal.

If no, it means you need to keep searching because you haven't found it yet.

Remember your goal starts before the scene even begins and isn't complete until the scene is over, and your goal doesn't change.

Be careful to not just repeat your goal as a broken record when doing this exercise. It is incredibly important for you to still hear the offers being made by the other characters in the actual text and to respond with authentic intentions. It is only the words you are changing here.

HEADSHOTS

HEADSHOTS

These are one of your most important marketing pieces and something you should never go cheap on. I am not saying always go with the most expensive photographer, but I am saying never let your headshots be "good enough." They should be great and an absolute representation of the real you or you shouldn't use them at all.

Here are some general rules when getting your headshots from selecting a photographer to selecting the final images you will use.

1. Find a photographer that has a portfolio of work you like. Know why you like it. Do they seem to capture the personalities of their clients? Is it the lighting? Is it the limited air brushing for a real effect? Is it the overall composition?
2. Involve your agent if you have one or other actor friends with headshots. Who do they recommend and why? You are not only the actor; you are the president of your company and in charge of research and development. Do your job or fire that person (i.e. you) for not getting the best out of your materials.
3. Be well rested and hydrated before the shoot. Seriously. And don't do anything else that day. Look rested and ready because you are rested and ready and don't be in a hurry to be somewhere else anytime soon. These can take a few hours and shouldn't be rushed. Enjoy the experience.
4. If the photographer doesn't mind, bring music you love that will relax you and put you in the right frame of mind.
5. Consider the differences and reasons behind shooting with natural light or studio light. Neither is right or wrong, but you should know why you want to shoot with either one of them.
6. Always look directly into the camera. I have a few special tricks I use when shooting, to make sure most of my shots are considerations when the shoot is complete. Remember you are likely shooting hundreds of shots and will need to go through them later. (1) I always have a secret in mind that is something I know the photographer would die to know. Whenever I look into the camera lens, I try to tell them this secret with only my eyes. It creates a magical look in your eyes that is authentic and leaves people wanting to know what you are thinking about. (2) I always avert my eyes from camera and only look into it when I am ready to shoot. This way the photographer isn't blindly shooting everything and hoping to catch something. We shoot when everything is ready. The lighting, the background, the eyes, the actor.

HEADSHOTS

7. Make this about you. Your eyes tell the story here. This means don't go crazy with make up, props, wardrobe, etc. Let you and your eyes be the most important part of the photoshoot and nothing else.

8. I like to always wear something that makes my eyes pop. I believe blue is always the best color for me so most of my shots have me in a blue a shirt. Make sure your clothes are clean and wrinkle free. It is sometimes tough to carry several outfits around for these shoots, but they need to look sharp and ready and not like you have been lugging them around all day in a tote bag. Layers can be effective but don't let it hide what you look like or your shape. Own every ounce of who you are and let these photos be authentic representations.

9. I recommend on aligning your headshots with everything else in your marketing package (demo reel and resume). Your looks should reflect your most popular hits or types you will go out for as an actor. Brooding teenager? Rebel? Professional? Agents and Casting Director will often want a shot with a smile, but don't let this be all you think about for this shot. What kind of roles do you think you'll go out for in commercials? And sure, you may be required to smile but as what type? Best friend? Professional? Rebellious Biker? Have your shots always represent you and what you will be seen as in this industry. We all want to be considered for everything and every character type. But you must first be something to someone before you can try to be everything to everyone.

10. Involve your agent, or friends if you aren't represented, in the selection process of picking your final two to three shots for print and use online. Don't make everyone go through all the photos. Narrow it down to your favorite twenty to thirty shots and then have people offer their input.

11. Casting will often look at breakdowns on a screen with multiple actor faces on it. Often five actors across and five down for twenty-five per page. What is it about your headshot that is going to make you be the one they select? Remember, no funny tricks or props, just good old-fashioned strategy and effort in this extremely important part of your marketing process.

12. As the world continues to move more and more towards everything being online, headshots are sometimes not required. Always have one with you. This doesn't mean you have to drop it off every time, particularly when they specifically ask you not to do so, but always have one just in case. Lots of people still prefer the tactile touch of the actual photo and resume.

RESUMES

In the beginning you may be tempted to use a very large font and double space everything. I know I did. But remember, we all start out with nothing and there isn't any shame here. Let your resume be a truthful representation of where you are and if you promise to commit to the craft it will get bigger and you will stop thinking about it.

There will also never be that elusive credit that once you get it, everything feels more legitimate. Be proud of the work you do, always seek to find new projects that expand your resume and your bank account, and smile knowing success is a journey and not a destination. There are lots of things you can put on your resume well before you book your first big gig. This document will be evolving throughout your entire career and there will possibly be a day where you need to start removing things from your resume. It'll be a weird feeling at first as we spend so much time trying to fill the page in the beginning, but if you work hard you will get there.

Here are some sections you can put on your resume in the early stages:

Training

This is big. If you don't have experience, you better have knowledge. Too many actors start with neither and wonder why their career never takes off. List the school or class, the instructor, and the dates you trained. Ideally, you have an item at the top of this list that reads "ongoing" as an end date, showing you are still working hard. Always put your most recent training at the top. There are examples in the following pages as references.

Theatre or Stage

Even high school stuff counts in the beginning. Name of the play, name of the role, name of the director and/or theatre company. Community theatre also works here in this column and is something you should be doing right now if you don't have a lot of performing experience. Often, these community theatre groups perform classic plays all actors should know, and they give chances to people to play epic roles from epic stories far before they are ready for the professional industry.

RESUMES

Special Skills

Only list special skills if they are actually special skills. If you kicked a soccer ball when you were nine in elementary school but haven't touched one since, I wouldn't list it. Do you have any military training or martial arts training? If yes, be specific and list active dates. Do you play any instruments? Which ones? For how long?

Have you won any awards for anything listed above? You can list it in its own section or clarify this next to where you have the credit already, in one of the sections already mentioned.

Resumes are typically formatted in three columns as you will see in the following pages.

You may list your agent and agent's contact information here somewhere at the top as well as your union number (if you have one) but you don't need to list anything else.

Your personal phone number, email, address, etc. can all go in a cover letter to prospective agents if you like, but they shouldn't be here.

If you write it on your resume, it had better be true.

There is nothing worse than having to come clean about lying about a special skill or having a fake credit exposed. Be real. It will all come in time if you do the work.

Film & Television

As you book television and film roles this will be where you will add most of your lines on your resume. This is always the top section if you have credits to fill in this area. For this section I recommend listing, in each of the three columns, the name of the project, the size of the role-category, and the director or network/production company.

Your agent will often help you here and even do this for you on their own letterhead. You will need a copy if this is the case so you can easily print them at home for auditions.

MICHAEL COLEMAN

Actor

UBCP #2443 /ACTRA #V01-06313

TALENT AGENCY

Agent: Jeff Smith (778) 222-8677

FILM

The Doctor's Case	Lead	Barkerville Productions
Thirty-Seventeen	Lead	Hadron Films & Rebel West
The Prodigals	Supporting	Sociable Films
Goners (Short)	Lead	Voice of Treason Productions
Puppet Killer	Supporting	Twisted Twins Productions
Last Night in Suburbia	Supporting	Suburban Pictures
Best Day Ever	Supporting	Best Film Ever Productions
Blood: A Butcher's Tale	Supporting	Pacific Gold Entertainment
Open Relationship	Lead	MM Original Productions
Alien Ops: Incursion	Supporting	Way Below the Line
The heart of Whistler (Short)	Supporting	Voice of Treason
Breakdown (Short)	Supporting	Fen 10 Films
Empty Orchestra (Short)	Lead	Grey Area Media
Masters of the Sea (Short)	Supporting	Grey Area Media
Inconvenience (Short)	Supporting	Zocalo Films
The Delicate Art of Parking	Supporting	Anagram Pictures
The Darkest Hour	Supporting	Movie House Pictures
Ark (Animated)	Supporting	Koko Productions
A Tree of Palm (Animated)	Supporting	ADV Films
Air Bud: Air Bud Spikes Back!	Supporting	Keystone Pictures
Dial "A" for Alphaman	Supporting	Space Network
A MidSummer's Nightmare	Supporting	OMNI Productions
The Water Game	Supporting	Freeform Productions
Just an Ordinary Day (Short)	Lead	Funnybone Productions
Memories of Sheldon	Lead	NISU Productions
The Total Package	Lead	Paragon Productions
I Knew You Were Waiting	Supporting	Paragon Productions

TELEVISION

Skylar	Series Regular	Skylar Productions Ltd.
Once Upon a Time	Recurring	ABC
Hipsterverse	Series Regular	Dish TV
King & Maxwell	Guest Star	TNT
Level Up	Guest Star	Cartoon Network
Smallville	Supporting	The CW
Fringe	Supporting	FOX
PSI: Paranormal Solutions Inc.	Recurring	Sociable Films
The Troop	Supporting	Nickelodeon
Stargate: Atlantis	Supporting	SyFy
Supernatural	Supporting	CW
Psych	Supporting	NBC
Blood Ties	Supporting	CHUM
Eureka	Supporting	SyFy
Stargate: SG-1	Supporting	MGM
The Triple Eight	Series Lead	Fast Productions
Point Blank	Recurring	Comedy Network
The Chris Isaak Show	Supporting	Showtime
My Guide to Becoming a Rockstar	Supporting	Warner Brothers
Almost Actors	Guest Star	Bitchpop Productions
DNG: The Series	Series Regular	Redrum
Identity Crisis	Series Regular	IC
Millennium	Supporting	FOX

MICHAEL COLEMAN

Actor

FILM

The Total Package	Lead	Paragon Productions
I Knew You Were Waiting	Supporting	Paragon Productions

TELEVISION

Millennium	Supporting	FOX

TELEVISION MOVIES

Honeymoon with Mom	Supporting	Lifetime
Y2K	Principal	NBC

TRAINING

Scene Study	Larry Moss	2015
Scene Study	Chris Fields	2014
Scene Study	Larry Moss	2013
Audition	Andrew Mcillroy	2008
Fraser Valley University	Theatre Program	1992

SPECIAL SKILLS

Singer (Tenor) – 6 years choir and multiple musical theatre stage performances
Wrestling (4 years) – BC High School Champion 1989
Ice Hockey (14 years)
Baseball (30+ years)

DEMO REELS

DEMO REELS

A demo reel is an introduction, speed dating version, and it lets people know what you look like on camera; what is your range, diversity, and character types, before they meet you in person or consider you for an audition or a role.

Ideally, your demo reel features you in "A" list films and series, acting brilliantly alongside some of the biggest names in the industry. But in the beginning this material often doesn't exist yet.

So it is advised you shoot an "Audition-style" demo reel. In the old days, we'd say shoot something funny and something serious. I see the merit in how this was decided but I respectively disagree with this concept. I advise filming two 2-minute scenes that showcase you playing two of your strongest "hits" (or character types you are most likely to play initially). Are you a young professional? Are you more military or police detective? Are you more of a best friend type? Are you the romantic lead? Find two that you are most likely to read for and use material that is already written (plays, tv, or film) but avoid popular performances we will all inevitably compare you to here. Make sure it is well lit, the sound is professional, and the camera work is spot on. Then you can just worry about nailing your performance. Use everything you've learned from this book to ensure you are truly delivering an authentic performance. You make first impressions once and you want them to be memorable for the right reasons. This demo should only be 2-4 minutes long. Let the demo end before the viewers interest does.

Once you have established professional credits you can create a more traditional demo that features your professional work on camera. Always start with your face if possible and end this way too. Lead off with your best scene and end with your second-best scene. Start hot, end hot. Only your best footage needs to be here. And remember this is an introduction, not a complete works library of everything you've done. Your performances will soon feel like they are your children and it will be hard to pick favorites. You need to be strong here and only pick what serves you. Leave them wanting more.

Today's software allows you to cut your own demos but there is still an art to be considered and I do recommend hiring a professional demo editor to ensure your reel is as strong and as effective as possible.

VOICE-OVER DEMOS

VOICE-OVER DEMOS

Some of the induration here is the same as the previous page regarding on-camera demo reels. Here are a few differences.

1. What tracks should you include and how long should each be?
2. Where do you get your content?
3. How should this be delivered?

It is important to remember that this is a subjective industry. All advice, including every word in this book is subjective. There aren't any hard, fast rules on what can or can't be done. If you always remember what the purpose of the voice-over demo is you really can't go wrong. This isn't your everything, it's your "best of" introduction demo.

1. Keep the total length short enough that people will actually listen.
2. Spend time on the performances not just the funny voices.
3. Only put your best stuff on the reel.

Here are some tracks to consider and information on building each:

Animation
This is where you can showcase your vocal range and abilities for cartoons and video games. The best approach is to cut together what sounds like a "best of" mash up of shows you are already on (not real shows but it will sound like real shows). Find the archetypes you can do (hero, crazy uncle, raspy villain, quirky weirdo, loveable sidekick, reluctant hero, evil master, etc.) and write 2-3 sentences of something they may say in an episode of something they might be in… make it up. You're creative. Have fun with this one! I would advise picking 12-16 voices and then have the audio engineer who mixes your demo add in some sfx and music to make it feel like it is from an actual episode. Remember your voice is what we're wanting to hear so don't bury it behind effects and music. Avoid saying things like "Arrr! This be me pirate voice!" A pirate would never say that. Think of something your character would actually say. Remember this is where casting directors are listening for range and ability. These voices should sound active and in a scene. Play with volume, emotion, scenario, everything until you find something that is engaging for us to listen to as an audience.

VOICE-OVER DEMOS

Commercials

Voicing commercials for radio and television and the internet can be a very lucrative and fun way to make a living or pay the bills while you are waiting for fame to happen as a film or television actor. On the next two pages you will find what I label as the **8 tones of selling**. One could argue that commercials break down into the hard sell or the soft sell, but I have found this categorization a much more useful way to articulate the types in my professional experience.

You can find the copy for the commercial by going to magazine ads or onto the web sites of various products and services. Almost all of these are written like radio ads. Remember this is just your demo and it isn't going to air anywhere, so make changes if necessary, to better suit what you want to do with each read. I would advise 3-5 samples of your three strongest tones. Remember again, this isn't your all-inclusive library of range. I am confident you can do most of them or all of them, but what are your BEST ones right now? What will get you in the room? Those should be on your demo. Each ad can be as short as 15 seconds and you can record them as one mash up of radio ads or as separate, labeled tracks on your demo.

Narration

I advise two types here, one being a technical read such you would do for an industrial video or perhaps a biography or a technical information video. The other I would read from a storybook or something similar. Both need to sound interesting and you need to be interested in whatever you are reading, always. These reads can each be about thirty to sixty seconds long for this track or tracks.

Singing

Are you a singer? What do you sing? Add songs, or a mash of songs here on your voice-over demo. If you sing a wide range of styles, include them! These can be acapella or with back tracks. You can also include a few jingles if you like and if you think this may be a strength of yours.

My advice for delivery is to have a link available to your voice-over demo and all of its tracks, and you can send this to potential agents or casting opportunities. These tracks can also live on your web site or some of the casting services web sites for easier access for those who want to give you a listen.

The 8 Tones of Selling

Best Friend – The idea here is to make sure you are using the warmth, familiarity, trustworthiness you would use when talking to a good friend. Get them to buy it for the same reasons you would buy it.

"Hey! You know how you and I are so similar and like the same things? Check out this thing I bought. It's exactly the kind of thing we like!"

Hip & Cool – This is a unique feeling where you care and don't care at the same time. You have so much confidence in how great your product or service is that you don't need to even try. Don't TRY to sell them. This level of indifference is a unique skill.

"Wanna buy these $150 jeans? You don't need to, as I am sure your $30 jeans are cool too. Not everyone needs to have $150 jeans."

Expert – The confidence of experience and education. This is when you know something so well you could teach it to others. Think "9 out of 10 dentists" and "tire experts" etc. Get them to buy based on your confidence and expertise.

"We asked 9 out of 10 dentists, you know people who've dedicated their entire LIFE to teeth, and asked them what toothpaste they recommend and use..."

Fear – This is where you scare people into buying your product or service and play on their fears. We often see this in financial, military, home security, medicine... They key here is to basically scare them into buying.

"Buy this product or suffer the potential consequences."

The 8 Tones of Selling

Health & Fitness – This high energy and positive read should sound infectious. When people hear it they should want to feel as energized and as positive as the person delivering the message. This has lots of "smile" and enthusiasm.

"Buy this thing and you could feel as amazing as I do RIGHT NOW!"

Seduction – This is exactly what it sounds like. It is seductive pillow talk. This is how we often sell chocolate or tantalizing treats, or shampoo that makes us feel wonderful, or anything that stimulates our pleasure sense. This is often under the category of "sex sells" but it's more than that. It's about teasing and tempting and indulging in pleasure more than anything else.

Comedy – This one is simple. Make me laugh. For real. Get the laugh.

"We would like to take this time to congratulate all of those that used our 'competitor's products'... Happy Father's Day. Durex condoms. What will you be wearing this holiday?"

Family – This is like the Best Friend read but more PG. This still has lots of smile in it but with a touch of "gosh, golly, gee" too. Think of it as Best Friend but Grandma is in the room, so you are using that "family" voice. Vacations, mini vans, cookies, cereal,... these are all samples of products that use this tone.

"I'm a busy Mom/Dad and I don't always have time to cook...."

AGENTS

AGENTS

For decades now I have heard the debate "Do you work for your agent or does your agent work for you?" I don't believe either is true, or technically, both are true.

Here are some things to consider when seeking an agent or considering a change in your representation:

Agents don't make any money unless you do. Often, they work for you 50+ hours a week for months or years, for free, until you start booking. Would you do this role? I know I wouldn't. This sounds hard and often thankless. AND... when you do book a role? They receive (15% in Canada and 10% in the US) of the money and you get all the credit and the remaining money. If someone offers to represent you, I think this is an incredible gesture on their part as a business partner and we should never disrespect the commitment they make out the gate.

So, how do you know who to "partner with" or "have represent you" in this industry? It really isn't unlike most relationships. While you will sit down with an agent and interview this is really a 2-way interview to see if both parties think this is a fit.

Do you both see yourself the same way in terms of potential, current abilities, character types? Do you guys align on short-term and long-term goals for your career? Do you have a feeling of mutual trust and respect? What are you each going to do to ensure the relationship continues to grow and be healthy for everyone involved? This is where you need to assess what you are willing to do. Will you continue training? Will you keep your headshots and demo reels current? Will you consider expanding your special skills to create more opportunities?

Your agent will secure audition opportunities through submissions, they will negotiate your contract for bookings, coordinate your audition and on-set schedules and keep in constant communication with you the actor. They will do a lot. Will you match or exceed their efforts? You will have loads of opportunities for obstacles from "money is tight" to "my day job doesn't let me have nights off to train" to "whatever." Be stronger than your excuses. Do you want this? Then go get it and always be the hardest working person on your team.

GLOSSARY

Blocking – This refers to the choreography of a scene. Where and when certain actions, dialogue, and movement occur.

Business – These are the non-spoken physical activities of the actor. What they are doing during a scene. This might be anything from reading a book to getting dressed for work to folding laundry to any action that helps create a more believable environment.

Monologue – A speech given by a single character in a play, movie, or television show.

Sides – These refer to the specific lines and scene(s) from a script an actor is asked to learn for their audition.

Thematic Premise – What is the main story about? What is it asking us to think about or what is it telling us it thinks and what we should do about it?

sfx– Sound effects. The audio added afterwards to compliment and enhance environment for the vocal tracks.

ACTIONS YOU CAN DO TO PEOPLE

Sample Tactics

Question	Interview	Interrogate	Examine	Grill	Investigate
Hurt	Burn	Sting	Squeeze	Stab	Spank
Hug	Embrace	Nurse	Love	Cradle	Welcome
Threaten	Scare	Abuse	Push	Caution	Spook
Thank	Praise	Bless	Reward	Honor	Stroke
Tease	Tempt	Taunt	Bait	Seduce	Tickle
Beg	Urge	Ask	Beseech	Nag	Press
Envy	Resent	Covet	Pinch	Poke	Punch
Appreciate	Recognize	Validate	Notice	Revere	Adore
Choose	Glorify	Admire	Treasure	Worship	Canonize
Criticize	Castigate	Lambaste	Condemn	Trash	Clobber
Flatter	Humor	Charm	Con	Glorify	Sweet-Talk
Ignore	Neglect	Evade	Reject	Scorn	Overlook
Discredit	Minimize	Undervalue	Roast	Depreciate	Pan
Develop	Boost	Enhance	Raise	Promote	Strengthen
Depress	Halt	Exhaust	Dwindle	Wilt	Reduce
Delight	Thrill	Awaken	Incite	Rouse	Jolt
Cheer	Inspire	Bolster	Comfort	Lift	Hearten
Rattle	Chill	Floor	Frighten	Fluster	Shake
Relieve	Pacify	Soften	Appease	Settle	Help

BE
STRONGER
THAN YOUR
— EXCUSES —

Dream Big.

Live Bigger.

STORY INSTITUTE

Dream Big. Live Bigger.

ACTING   MUSIC CREATION   WRITING

MISSION STATEMENT

Creative professionals will share the classic
fundamentals and the modern techniques needed
to succeed in today's industry that they themselves
use in their own successful careers.

STORY INSTITUTE
320 – 640 W. Broadway
Vancouver, BC V5Z 1G4
(778) 222-8677
Storyinstitute.ca

Feel free to reach out to Michael directly at michaelcoleman@storyinstitute.ca

Acting made me happy, who do you want to be?

About the Author

Michael is the founder of Story Institute a post-secondary school for the creative arts. In addition to his 25+ years working as a professional actor, writer, producer, Michael has been a leading innovator in professional arts education.

Michael has trained with different coaches from New York, Los Angeles, and Vancouver.

Michael is a principal and founder of Rebel West Pictures and he has created numerous projects for both film and television.

Michael has worked steadily in animation, on stage, and on screen, winning several awards as a writer and as an actor. Some of his more notable credits include Once Upon a Time, Stargate: Atlantis, Stargate: SG-1, The Doctor's Case, Supernatural, Hello Kitty, Dragonball Z, Thirty-Seventeen, Stargate, Hamataro, Far Cry 3, Inuyasha, Hipsterverse, Smallville, and Megaman: NT Warrior.

In addition to the colorful and iconic characters I've been grateful to play on film and television I am equally thrilled with my opportunity to share what I've learned with hundreds of actors who have been able to achieve and exceed their own goals. Seeing actors I've worked with go on to play leads and supporting roles on projects like Riverdale, The Chilling Adventures of Sabrina, My Little Pony, Lego Star Wars, Barbie. The 100, The Handmaid's Tale, and so many others has become equally rewarding.

Never let your inner brat convince you that you are not good enough. Never let others who gave up on their dreams, convince you to give up on your dreams.

Manufactured by Amazon.ca
Bolton, ON

10803660R00071